FLANNELLED FOOL AND MUDDIED OAF

Peter West was an outstanding sportsman at school but his adult career has been devoted to providing insights from the side-lines. He has been a household name since the mid-1950s when his appearances on a variety of television shows made him a focus of attention that he would sometimes rather have done without. It may surprise many to learn that he was once of the subject of a *News of the World* headline which screamed 'Peter West in Nude Swim Party!' The story behind this and many other fascinating incidents is here told with the skill and good humour we have come to expect of this consummate broadcasting professional.

D1553955

FLANNELLED FOOL AND MUDDIED OAF

The Autobiography of Peter West

A STAR BOOK
published by
the Paperback Division of
W. H. Allen & Co. Plc

A Star Book
Published in 1987
by The Paperback Division of
W. H. Allen & Co. Plc
44 Hill Street, London W1X 8LB

First published in Great Britain by
W. H. Allen & Co. Plc in 1986

Copyright © Peter West, 1986

Printed and bound in Great Britain by
Anchor Brendon Ltd, Tiptree, Essex

ISBN 0 352 32093 1

For Paul
who always keeps the home fires burning
and never complains when the breadwinner
is away on the road

Then ye returned to your trinkets;
    then ye contented your souls
with the flannelled fools at the wicket
    or the muddied oafs at the goals.

Rudyard Kipling

Introduction

WHY ANYONE SHOULD want to read a book by an author who
has been referred to in the press as being bland, boring,
childish, cliché-ridden, cloying, colourless, deferential,
fatuous, futile, gauche, half-baked, ill at ease, impolite,
ingratiating, nauseating, officious, overbearing, peremp-
tory, pious, pompous, prejudiced, prim, rude, sugar-sweet,
squirming, tiresome, twittering, unappealing, unconvincing
and unctuous, I am not at all sure.

On the other hand, I have been described as affable,
bluff, charming, cheerful, confident, debonair, decisive,
equable, firm, gentle, knowledgeable, masterly, personable,
pleasant, polite, popular, professional, robust, sporty, tact-
ful, tough, versatile, unbiased, unobtrusive and unruffled.

Most paid-up members of the great viewing fraternity will
have long since made their choice.

I ought to add that in a career spanning four decades in
front of a microphone or a camera, most of the unwanted
epithets were collected when working on television programmes unconnected with sport. Others, to which I shall
allude later, have been acquired courtesy of enraged or
apoplectic viewers. It would be self-indulgent as well as
boring to dwell on the bouquets. The raspberries may be
more entertaining.

No doubt I would have avoided much of the flak by concentrating on cricket and rugby, or at least on sport as a

whole. But struggling to establish myself as a broadcaster in the early fifties I found, alas, that as a free-lance (which I have always remained) I could not get enough sporting assignments to support one wife and three young children in the style to which I ambitiously aspired.

A chance meeting with C. B. Fry, in 1947, was one turning point in my life: it unlocked the door to a career as a cricket commentator which at that time I had never thought to take up. It gave me a tenuous foothold on a radio ladder the higher rungs of which were firmly occupied in those days by luminaries such as Rex Alston, John Arlott, Jim Swanton and Brian Johnston.

Over the next few years, thanks mainly to the support of the old B.B.C. West Region, I cut my teeth and began to learn the trade as a radio commentator. But seeing little chance of being invited to join the Test match panel I sought to make my way in what was then a relatively new medium. In the spring of 1953, when I had been installed for some time as a TV commentator at Test matches and rugby internationals (but still wondered where the rent was coming from at other times), Eamonn Andrews turned another key.

Jerry Desmonde had fallen ill, unable to appear on the panel of 'What's My Line?'. In its halcyon days, when there was one television channel, and Gilbert Harding crossed swords with Eamonn as well as with some of the contestants, it made for compulsive viewing and many column inches in Monday's newspapers. On Eamonn's recommendation a brave producer, T. Leslie Jackson, threw this Christian, for one night only, to the lions.

The art of a panellist, Eamonn has sagely observed, lies in a capacity to think quickly on one's seat. Given swift mental reaction he or she must of course also have the confidence to relax, to concentrate on every word and to enjoy the experience. 'Don't worry,' Gilbert said in his most avuncular vein, 'we'll look after you.' There was similar encouragement from Eamonn as well as the other panellists, Barbara Kelly and Ghislaine Alexander. Much good did it do a petrified new boy.

I must have done rather better than I had feared. Soon afterwards I was offered the chair of a new panel game, 'Why?', Roy Plomley having first declined it because he was indisposed. Mr Plomley, his 'Desert Island Discs' programme already well established, may have been wiser than he knew. His death in 1985 deprived the B.B.C. of its most courteous, gentle knight.

By public and critical demand 'Why?' bit the dust after three programmes, but yet again I was reprieved. While most of the panellists unfortunate enough to appear on it disappeared temporarily from view, the chairman was retained to handle the reins of yet another game, 'Guess My Story', which featured contestants in the recent news. This one, happily, was more to the general liking. It ran for three series.

By now, whether or not my face fitted, it was becoming familiar in the nation's parlours and, rather grandly as it seemed to me at the time, I was dabbling round the fringes of show-biz and had acquired a personal manager to handle my affairs. Exposure being the name of the game, Edward Sommerfield concluded a deal whereby my smiling visage, along with that of the far more appealing film actress, Susan Shaw, would appear, teeth rendered whiter than white, in a dentifrice advertisement.

Any inhibitions modestly entertained about this exercise were swiftly banished when my manager mentioned the fee, which was comfortably in excess of the rewards to be garnered from five days' work at a Test match. All this and heaven, too, as the result of an hour's session with a photographer. I was now hooked – for better or for worse – on a wider-ranging career.

In the course of the next twenty years or so I worked for every department of B.B.C. Television except Drama. The Outside Broadcasts Department kept me occupied from the mid-fifties not just on rugby and cricket, but at Wimbledon, as the poor man's Dan Maskell on No. 1 Court, on Olympic or Commonwealth Games and on more than thirty sports all told.

9

For Outside Broadcasts I did a number of 'At Home' programmes featuring the middle or working classes while that doyen and supreme professional, Richard Dimbleby, presided over those involving the Establishment. For a number of series I introduced a programme about animal pets called 'Good Companions', with Stanley Dangerfield as the acknowledged expert. This put its main emphasis on dogs, which may have a few nasty habits but can be relied on, for the most part, to exhibit winsome reactions when confronted by a camera. Dogs also reveal the most remarkable loyalty and good cheer even after you have been beastly to them. The same cannot be said about cats, self-sufficient creatures who tend to treat you in similar circumstances with understandable hauteur.

Dogs never let us down on 'Good Companions', the only programme I have ever done on television without getting an abusive letter. Wilfred Pickles, concentrating his attentions on animals with four legs or human beings over eighty with two, must have known what he was doing.

I appeared once, I would have you know, with Malcolm Muggeridge on 'Panorama'. This suggests a touch of class although the subject of my contribution, Les Bluebell Girls of Gay Paree, may indicate something else. I anchored 'Get Ahead' (about business entrepreneurs), and 'First Hand' (eyewitness testimony to historic events such as the sinking of the *Titanic*). I presented a holiday programme, reflecting British stoicism in adversity, called 'Wish You Were Here', and refrained, when the rains bucketed down in Morecombe and everywhere else, from suggesting how lucky you weren't.

I was one of several so-called personalities playing the role of Buttons in a self-indulgent 'Pantomania' screened at Christmas time. I endeavoured to dance a televised tango with Lulu. I introduced up-and-coming talent shows for the B.B.C.'s northern impresario, Barney Colehan. One Saturday evening in the days B.C. (Before Commercial), I was the commentator when – would you believe it? – small bore shooting from Salisbury Plain was the B.B.C.'s peak time television offering. This produced the not surprising comment from a critic that it had been the biggest bore of the night.

For many years I was associated with a schools programme, 'Going To Work', which I found immensely satisfying and rewarding in more senses than one. It was *repeated*, which involved an extra fee and that was more than could be said for one's efforts at a Test match, odd items of which at one time might later be transmitted throughout a fading Empire for another sixteen and sixpence – and later still for nothing at all.

For some years I covered, metaphorically speaking, 'Miss World', a long-running saga assured of a vast audience but subsequently lost by the B.B.C. to I.T.V. The compere of this show is on a hiding to nothing: what in many ways is a harmless and entertaining exercise carries undertones of a public auction. It is not easy to ask the contestants to turn about in unison – in order that their bottoms may be regarded – without attracting the critics' scorn.

It was satisfying to overcome the challenge presented by a live programme but I did not much enjoy the experience. Interviewing the finalists could be a taxing task if their knowledge of the Queen's English was limited or nonexistent. However, I managed eventually to get myself released from this chore. Michael Aspel took charge of the chat, impressing everyone with his versatility by posing questions in the appropriate language. I don't think he understood a word of the replies he got, but it all sounded extremely impressive. I introduced six Miss World shows on the box, which was more, I think, than anyone else had managed at that time. Then someone must have realized that I was almost old enough to be her grandfather, and Simon Dee took over. Whatever happened to him?

I have left mention of 'Come Dancing' to the last in this introduction since that is the one programme, for good or ill, with which I was longest identified on TV. As the world's worst and most reluctant dancer – my wife wears shin pads – I may have been the biggest fraud on the box.

It is fourteen years since I voluntarily withdrew from the longest-running programme on television, but the public still remind me of it with some regularity. To that extent I feel it is a cross I have to carry through my life, though I suppose I ought to feel flattered that after all this time I am still identified with the show. Never mind. By opting out of the programme – and sadly ending a long association with its producer, Barrie Edgar – at least I got the Scots off my back. It seemed that whenever Scotland were beaten in 'Come Dancing' many of its inhabitants held me personally responsible. I was regarded as their biggest scourge since Edward the Hammer.

It ought not to be overlooked by students of TV form that my departure from 'Come Dancing' provided an opportunity for a promising Irish lad to get himself the regular TV exposure he was then seeking. I had to admit that Terry Wogan had more hair.

It was not Terry's scene to work to a more or less set script. On 'Come Dancing' he never quite seemed at ease. But lo, what wonders his beguiling wit and charm wrought for 'Blankety Blank', which surely needed them, and then for the Wogan chat show, on which from its outset he ran the obvious risk of over-exposure.

These were varied and mostly happy days. I was Jack of all trades, master of none. But this flannelled fool and muddied oaf, seeking some respectability in his declining years, became rugby correspondent of *The Times* and reverted, in television, to doing just those things he had sought to do in the first place.

If I have a regret, it is that because of my commitments as a free-lance I have never travelled on a cricket tour or on a major rugby expedition overseas. I was lucky enough to cover three short England rugby tours for *The Times* and B.B.C. Radio. I was willing to forgo a summer's cricket broadcasting to cover, for my newspaper, the Lions' tour of

New Zealand in 1977. All but one of the other national newspapers dispatched their correspondents to cover this apogee of British rugby but *The Times*, for reasons of economy, decided not to send theirs. I was ready – and my arrangements had the blessing of Jonathan Martin, an understanding head of B.B.C. TV Sport – to cover all but a few matches of the next Lions' tour to New Zealand in 1983. Yet again *The Times* said no. This struck me as being an astonishing decision by an organ purporting to cover the game of rugby seriously. For this and other reasons I resigned in protest.

In his superb autobiography, *My Life and Soft Times*, the late Henry Longhurst reflected how fortunate he had been to cover his chosen sport, golf, for a paper and a television service happy to dispatch him round the world at their expense. I have travelled less widely than Henry, but I have seen a lot of interesting places while someone else has picked up the tab. On the parochial front I count myself lucky to have had a free ticket to many sporting occasions and to be the envy of my sporting friends.

I can remember my excitement when as a young agency reporter in 1946 I was dispatched to Taunton to cover a Somerset–Gloucestershire cricket match with orders to gather some details from the visiting captain, the one and only Walter Hammond.

He had been one of my heroes, worshipped from afar, in the thirties. I can see him now, silk shirt ruffling those broad shoulders, striding out to bat for Gloucestershire and England like a ship under full sail. I never thought in those days that I would have the privilege of talking to the great man.

On the last day of the Taunton encounter I knocked on his dressing room door, was bidden to enter and said, with a respect amounting to reverence: 'Sir, my sports editor has asked if you can tell me your side for the next fixture.'

'Fuck off,' my hero replied. And that ended my one and only conversation with him.

13

The manuscript of this book went to the printers last January, shortly before the England cricket team flew to the Caribbean for their tour of the West Indies. It is inevitable that some of the things I have written have been overtaken by events.

My indulgent publishers have enabled me, at page-proof stage, to add some further paragraphs in which I first mourn the passing of two old friends, Jim Laker and Bill Edrich. This last chapter includes some thoughts about the troubled world of rugby union and, within its corridors of power, the turmoil which has ensued as a result of the unoffical tour made by Andy Dalton's New Zealand Cavaliers to South Africa. Having witnessed all of their matches up to and including the first international, I can report on part of that expedition at first hand.

The decision of the International Rugby Board, at its meeting in April, to permit players, coaches, referees and administrators, once their active careers are finished, to accept fees for their contributions to the media is another thing that has made my earlier comments now out of date.

Finally, I have had the chance to write something about that traumatic England cricket tour and to add, on earlier pages, a paragraph or two about David Gower and Ian Botham, who has parted company with his flamboyant manager, Tim Hudson.

Chapter One

AN OBSESSIVE INTEREST in sport had not been inherited from my parents although my father, without ever understanding the game's finer points, came to be hooked on televised cricket in his old age. I have always tended first to scan the headlines of a newspaper, then to turn to the sport and read the pages from back to front. My father focused his prime attention on the financial news – an interest which went back to his early days in the City of London where he had done well enough in the oil business to be able to bid it farewell before he was thirty. He had an excellent head for figures, not, I may say, inherited by his offspring, and I think in those days he was dabbling in the stock market with considerable flair and success.

He was a tobacconist's son who had left school at the age of fifteen. What he missed in formal education he more than made up for by his avid reading – which was one reason, no doubt, why he wrote impeccable English. I treasured the long letters, humorous and replete with wisdom, which he regularly sent to me at boarding school, and I only wish now that I had kept them.

I was four years old when in 1924 he abandoned a successful City career for the country life. He bought a substantial gabled house outside Cranbrook, amongst the hop fields and orchards of Kent in the Garden of England, and on the thirty or so acres that went with it set himself up as a poultry farmer. He was not a man to do things by halves. For several years, until it all but broke him, the job consumed his waking hours.

Few hints of his problems were apparent to a small boy collecting his tadpoles, snaring butterflies, riding on the back of a gentle, accommodating cow named Milky, and being introduced to cricket by a Mr Chapman. My first cricketing tutor expounded the virtues of playing with a straight bat and if an early photograph of my exaggerated forward defensive stroke is any guide, I was over-coached from a tender age. I made the same sort of mistake when my own two lads came to hold a bat, although I had the sense to decree that the younger one should be a left hander when he adopted a cack-handed stance. In their tenderest years boys should be encouraged – given a proper grip of the bat handle – simply to hit the ball and enjoy the experience. Technique can be acquired later. Having said that, I remain eternally grateful to Mr Chapman for nourishing in my heart a love for a lovely game.

My father adored my mother, a petite, vivacious woman and a beauty in her youth. She was far more gregarious and outgoing than her husband and I am sure that when they moved to the country she missed her old friends and the social life of the big city. However, the acquisition of a Chrysler de Soto, which was quite a flashy motorcar in those days, enabled her in the late twenties to keep in touch with her parents and maintain old contacts. Her father, a retired quartermaster sergeant from the Royal Horse Artillery, was a Welsh-speaking Williams from Montgomeryshire. I like to ascribe my love of rugby football to him, but in truth he never mentioned the game in my presence. I doubt indeed if he ever saw it played.

I remember what a thrill it was being driven to see my grandparents who lived at Addiscombe, near Croydon. The de Soto reached the dizzy speed of sixty m.p.h. and got half-way up Goudhurst Hill, five miles from Cranbrook, without a need to come down a gear. The smallest car now takes that hurdle in easeful stride, but it was exciting then to reach the oak tree in top. Less exhilarating was the requirement in winter to wrap up the feet against a danger of frost bite.

The older my mother got the more endearingly vain she became about her age. She was four years older than my father, as she reluctantly had to admit to me when I found out the secret one day, and even into her sixties and early seventies, when she remained wonderfully well-preserved – and looked years younger – she stubbornly declined to reveal the truth in public. Repeated family suggestions by sundry generations that her looks belied her age – which might therefore have been taken as a striking compliment – consistently fell on deaf ears.

I am sure she spoiled her only child. I do not blame her for so human a weakness but I regret not having had brothers or sisters to knock off some complacent and selfish edges. I was much closer to her in my formative years partly because my father's energies were so taken up with the farm but also because he was a man not easy to know intimately. As the years rolled by I came to regard him with a greater yet still rather distanced affection and respect. Any failure to communicate may have been as much my fault as his. I dare say my own children have had the same problems when dealing with their stubborn father. Mine was sensitive, selfless and extremely generous. He embodied some old and timeless virtues.

In the autumn of 1929 he sent me as a nine-year-old boarder to Yardley Court, an admirable preparatory school in Tonbridge many of whose pupils moved on in due course to the senior Tonbridge school. He had intended that I should be one of them but, unknown to me then, he was fighting a losing battle as a small-time farmer. By 1931, at the height of a world-wide recession, he had reached the limit of his financial resources and was compelled to sell out at an horrendous loss. It was an expensive experience from which he was to make a courageous recovery, but it left its scars.

There was no way he could afford to keep me at Yardley Court but he found a happy alternative closer to hand. In the thirties the boarding fees at Cranbrook School were about £75 a year; day boys paid £12. For two terms I joined its ranks as a day boy. When my parents moved to a modest new home in Ewhurst, Surrey, they somehow scraped enough together to keep me at Cranbrook as a boarder, but my father, now facing a slow and difficult return to City life, could not afford this luxury for long. The headmaster, aware of his difficulties, arranged for me to sit the scholarship examination during the following summer term. I achieved the top award of £60.

Founded in 1518, known from later in that century as Queen Elizabeth's Grammar School and retaining a charter from good Queen Bess to prove it, Cranbrook is, I believe, unique in one respect. There are three more Cranbrook Schools in the world, all of them founded by men who started their lives in the capital of the Kentish Weald. One of them, in Michigan, was inaugurated by a George C. Booth, whose father had been a tin and coppersmith in Cranbrook, Kent. Another is in Sydney and a third in the Rocky Mountains of Canada. When a party of American Cranbrookians came on an official visit to the alma mater in 1936, I remember how impressed we were to learn that most of the senior day boys drove to school in their own cars.

In 1932 there were only about 130 boys at the English Cranbrook although its numbers were almost to double and its amenities to increase significantly under the influence of a new headmaster. This was C. Russell Scott, a nephew of C. P. Scott, distinguished editor of the old *Manchester Guardian*. His reign at Cranbrook extended for thirty-one fruitful years including those of the war when no other public school stayed closer to Hitler's guns and aircraft. If the Luftwaffe threatened danger, Cranbrook's headmaster, who had learned to play the bugle while a boy at Haileybury, had his own alarm system.

In those days it was not the fashion to appoint young

18

headmasters. Russell Scott, then only thirty-one, got the Cranbrook appointment in 1929 when an innovative broom was clearly needed. It was revealed in the next term's magazine that his predecessor 'had been compelled to resign'.

Years afterwards I was told how the previous headmaster had opened some School Certificate papers and provided his pupils with some useful coaching in advance of the examination. The whole miserable episode came to light when the vice-master, one Major Saunders, commander and pillar of the Officers' Training Corps, had satisfied himself that the rumour was truth, and forthwith reported the matter to the governors. It was later discovered, moreover, that the headmaster had made a habit of purchasing text books from the local education authority at a discount before selling them to the school at the published prices. All such seamy details were unknown to an eleven-year-old when he arrived for his first term as a day boy in January 1932.

If it is broadly true that most of the memorable books about school life seem to have been written by those who found the experience horrific or degrading, let me supply an unmemorable paragraph by declaring that I remember my years at school with feelings – in the main – of warmth and affection. No doubt I was lucky: in many ways I never had it so good.

Russell Scott was a brilliant headmaster to whom in my formative years I owed a considerable debt: a wise and tolerant man, genuinely humble, without a hint of self-importance. He transformed the school's academic standards. He had exceptional gifts as an administrator and a passion for music, notably Mozart, which, alas, this philistine never came to appreciate or share. He was founder of the Cambridge Council for Musical Education and the Committee for Music and Drama in the Villages of England. His broad vision led to the creation of some outstanding youth orchestras.

A quiet, sometimes mischievous sense of humour

inspired him to include in his end-of-term reports such comments as 'he can concentrate for seconds on end', or 'the dawn of legibility in his handwriting has revealed a total inability to spell'. I am sorry to report that although he was known as Rollo to his family and intimate friends, the boys crudely referred to him as Shovit on account of his ever-growing family. Not that they were ungrateful to get a half-holiday to mark the new arrivals.

Perceptive selections of staff were not the least of his accomplishments: in the thirties he attracted to the masters' common room some men richly diverse in talent and approach. There was Bernard ('Bill') Jaeger, a Radleian with an open scholarship to Cambridge who came to Cranbrook to teach languages. An unconventional but never eccentric character, he loved hunting and riding and lived with his horse in the stables of a demolished house where he would frequently play host to boys devoted to him. Disdaining the creature comforts of life, he joined the RAF in 1942 and two years later was posted 'missing' while serving as a sergeant navigator in a Mosquito.

Ubaldo Gianetti, head of modern languages, was described by his headmaster as a seagreen incorruptible. Yet his gentle nature seemed transformed when, as a referee of junior rugby games, he would use his whistle's lanyard to whip the backsides of slothful performers. To the delight of his classes he would often perch himself on the front of his desk wth fly buttons still undone. He was to die in harness in the early sixties when nearing retirement.

Anthony Congreve, a direct descendant of the dramatist, enriched the school in a variety of ways, loyally and unstintingly coaching the cricket and rugby colts for many years, preparing the seeds for others to harvest and never getting the credit. 'Pop' Osborne, a wise little man, barely five feet tall, with a bald, glistening pate, presided over history and rapidly concluded that this author, after arriving in the upper sixth form, had no pretensions to University scholarship status in his own subject. I did not much care for him when I was at school, nor he for me. But time, in my case, has mellowed a young, impulsive judgement. He sought to open a shuttered mind.

The chemistry and physics master, Shirley Wheatcroft, mixed a sarcastic tongue with a heart of gold. Perverse or ignorant pupils were required to advance from their desks and stand within range of his three-foot ruler, which he used to administer a painful crack on the ear at any further sign of errancy. So far as I know, it never did anyone any lasting harm and no one bore him a grudge. For men such as these, schoolmastering was a full-time occupation, to which they were wholly dedicated. I do not doubt that in today's best schools staff remain inspired by the same unselfish approach. It is one of the things parents still willingly pay for in independent education.

To the five members of staff I have mentioned can be added three more who were inherited by the headmaster from his predecessor. W. F. Griffin ('Griff') was a fervent Welsh housemaster who taught maths to a high level and was suspected of giving his house team pep pills before they played a rugby match. Such suspicion was wholly unworthy, but his team kept on winning and, until it did, Griff, running up and down the touchline, would die a thousand deaths. 'Mathematics,' he said to me once, 'is ten per cent common sense and ninety per cent guts. The trouble with you, West, is that you've got no guts.' When I achieved a credit in School Certificate it was a toss-up which of us was more surprised.

Major (subsequently Lt-Col) H. F. Saunders, the vice master, who was known as 'Sandy' or 'Dogs', ran for thirty-one years with a rod of iron what I am convinced was the finest and most efficient Officers Training Corps in England. He may not have been innovative or even up-to-date about military tactics but in turn-out, drill, general discipline and unit pride he surely had no peers. Our parades on speech days would have done credit to the Guards. We regularly received glowing reports after official

War Office inspections and our Commanding Officer took it for granted that Cranbrook would always win the Brigade Guard competition at OTC camps in the summer holidays.

As Sergeant of the Cranbrook guard destined to compete for the title at Oxney in 1938, I did not share his view about automatic success. I thought we needed all the rehearsal we could get. So, rather to the CO's disgust but without his outright opposition, we practised diligently in our spare time at the end of the summer term. At camp, everything went swimmingly until after the moment of our triumph.

All of us had splendidly burnished bayonets but none had a shinier one than the Sergeant. It was a prized Corps possession lovingly handed down by my predecessor. The unfortunate error I made was to put it in the fixed position for the official photograph when it ought to have been kept in its scabbard.

Arriving back at school for the start of a new term and my last year at Cranbrook, I was confronted by an irate Major holding the offending photograph in his hand. 'You bloody young fool,' he said. 'You've ruined the whole thing.' It must have been with the greatest reluctance that he sanctioned my promotion to Sergeant Major for the next twelve months.

'Dogs' Saunders held no academic degree but he had an abiding love for the works of William Shakespeare, inspiring many of his pupils to share it. He ran the dramatic society and staged productions with panache. His greatest triumph occurred in my last term, in 1939, when his shooting VIII won the Ashburton Shield at Bisley. At that time Cranbrook was the smallest school to acquire that trophy. It made for a happy end to a sporting year in which the rugby XV had finished unbeaten.

In days before the axe of Lord Beeching fell on British Railways, Cranbrook boasted a station on a branch line from Paddock Wood. A coal cart was dispatched to meet the Major and his conquering marksmen upon their return. The whole school, as well as most of the town's inhabitants, turned out to conduct them home – with the OTC band playing – on the last mile of their journey. I think we did the gallant Major proud.

It was clear that an officer never averse to the odd tipple had partaken of a few jars on the journey back from Bisley. He had several more that evening in the study of his old friend, Frank Evans, who was my housemaster. We could hear, from our dormitory above, the sounds of a bibulous celebration and then of a well-oiled Major setting uncertain course for base camp.

It was an even bet whether he or his corps storeman, 'Tug' Wilson, went more unsteadily to bed that night. Tug was another tremendous character. A former naval petty officer who came to Cranbrook from Eton's more rarefied stratum, he looked a dead ringer for Disney's Pop-Eye. He worshipped his commanding officer and the Cranbrook Corps, deploring its eventual translation to Junior Training Corps, and then to Combined Cadet Force. These he rightly saw as changes for the worse.

No master had a greater influence on my school days than Frank William Lucas Evans, a confirmed bachelor who was Cranbrook's Mr Chips. Arriving from Oxford in 1926 to take charge of Crowden House and the teaching of classics, he was still in his late twenties when I began as a boarder in the Christmas term of 1932. New boys stood in awe of a man with an imposing physical presence who was known as 'Lanky Joe' or just plain 'Joe'. With his squarish jowl, high forehead and close-cropped thinning thatch he could have adorned the ranks of Bismarck's Uhlans. In his relaxed, more amiable moments he looked not unlike the actor Alastair Sim. Joe was another who exemplified some old fashioned virtues: hard work and dedication, pride in the job, discipline, loyalty, honesty and a rock-like integrity.

Exuding a magisterial authority, he never experienced the slightest difficulty in maintaining discipline. He could be very fierce with anyone he thought dishonest, withering

23

with those he considered had let themselves, his house or Cranbrook down. So he was a firm upholder of the law and civilized behaviour at a time in our lives when we needed to know what was acceptable in a close-knit society and what was not. Above all, he was just. Even those who fell regularly foul of him had to admit that although he seemed a right old bugger, at least he was a fair one.

Some of us met with the ultimate deterrent. This was kept in his bookcase, behind the collected works of Ovid, and a beating was administered with the suggestion that it was paining him as least as much as it was hurting the victim. If that was the case, he must have suffered mental agonies. I can no longer remember what I was caned for, but I have no doubt I deserved it. It left nothing but temporary physical distress, and I never bore him the slightest resentment.

His study on the ground floor was awash with *Wisdens*, the works of Horace, and Gilbert and Sullivan records which he lovingly played for favoured pupils amidst tea and macaroons. His garret-like bedroom on the top floor had a less than inspiring view of the gasworks, but a more impressive one of Cranbrook's seven-storey windmill which, though no longer used, remains in good working order and is said to be the biggest and finest mill of its kind in England. He would take lunch with the boys of his house, and dinner with the headmaster and his family in School House where some members of the fairer sex – matrons, sisters, secretaries and the like – quite often got on his nerves. I am sure he consistently got on theirs.

Daily breakfast was served to him in solitary state in the dining hall. *The Times* would be propped up on the toast rack, and a glowering look would suffuse his noble countenance if he had got out of bed the wrong way or the Kent cricket team had endured a bad yesterday.

The length and variety of his devoted contributions to Cranbrook life were unique. He had charge of his house and of the classical teaching for forty years, consistently producing the highest record of success in school examinations to

PETER WEST

the then Higher Certificate level. He ran Cranbrook cricket
for thirty-two years without a break, and for thirty-five altogether. He ran the rugger for twenty-two, the hockey for
twenty-one, and the fives for all of his time at the school. He
had gone close to an Oxford Blue for hockey. At Cranbrook
he would play hockey on Big Side and referee at the same
time, barging wretched defenders out of his imperious path
and then penalizing them for obstruction.

For twenty years Joe held a commission in the OTC. He
commanded it for two and frightened the lives out of callow
young men with his stern, unyielding gaze and strident
parade commands of which Guards drill sergeants would
have been proud. He was chairman of the Literary and
Debating Society for twenty-two years. He made some
memorable contributions to sing-songs, and he did his bit
by the Dramatic Society, once playing the part of Stanhope
in *Journey's End* and looking and sounding, to universal
acclaim, exactly like himself. I must not omit to mention that
he was vice-master for his last fifteen years and acting headmaster, during a brief interregnum, in 1960.

As a devoted coach of games, Joe spent thousands and
thousands of selfless hours on Cranbrook's playing fields.
At fielding practice on wintry days in early May he would
propel the ball at his victims with an ancient, heavy bat.
'*Two* hands, you wretched boy, *two* hands . . .' I can hear
him now. But how well he implanted the basics, how grateful we were for being taught the virtues of playing straight
or bowling a decent length and line.

Length and line were the only merits of my attempted
off-breaks which showed few perceptible signs of spin and
in later years were regularly dispatched over the mid-wicket
boundary. However, they did get me my half-colours in my
first year in the XI. I mention this only because it happened
at Ardingly where several years earlier Cranbrook had
made 403 for six wickets (in a one-day game) and then left
themselves a mere two hours and twenty minutes to bowl
out their hosts. This they deservedly failed to do. If Joe had

a weakness as cricket coach, it was a failure to encourage his captains in a positive approach.

Joe's rugby coaching, in retrospect, seems to have been quite unsophisticated: the forwards were expected to win the ball, the scrum-half to shovel it out, the backs to run in tries. But in those days the game was different even at higher levels; under Joe we learned how to tackle, how to give and time and take a pass. It's a pity he couldn't have had a go at one or two England midfields of fairly recent memory.

I remember the day when for the first time we beat Sutton Valence School at rugger. We were leading by about thirty points when from the stand-off half position I tried a drop shot which missed by a mile. However, we won 40–4, having run in twelve tries, only two of which I managed to convert into goals. I approached the maestro, still expecting an accolade. 'Foolish boy,' he said, 'if you had, er, got the ball out instead of attempting that ridiculous drop, it would have been forty-five.'

There was an unprecedented attendance at the Old Cranbrookians' dinner marking Joe's retirement in 1966. Making amusing stories sound hilarious with a stilted, hesitant delivery but a masterly sense of timing, he brought the house down. 'For He's a Jolly Good Fellow' was sung with enormous fervour. After retiring from Cranbrook Joe went to live in Eastbourne, within handy reach of the Saffrons cricket ground. Robert Bairamian, headmaster of Holmewood House preparatory school in Tunbridge Wells, had the perception to engage him for some years as a part-time teacher of Latin and Greek, in which subjects he more than maintained that institution's fine academic record. I dare say he also contributed some wise thoughts about its sporting prowess.

At length, in the autumn of 1978, Joe was struck down by a terminal illness, cancer of the liver and bile duct. The surgeons gave him only a few weeks to live. But the tough old bird was made of sterner stuff. By the following Feb-

26

ruary, to the astonishment of his medicos, he had moved off to a nursing home, there to be installed with a television set for watching the rugby. In no time he was taking a daily walk, holding court again with Old Cranbrookians and friends. It seemed then that if he could continue to mock medical opinion he might be prevailed upon to attend one more Old Cranbrookians' dinner. So in due course it was arranged – entirely against medical advice. He journeyed to London by train, took an afternoon siesta at the Charing Cross Hotel and came to Simpson's in the Strand to meet his old boys for the last time. What is more he sank a bottle of claret before being amongst the last to leave at around midnight.

This was an astonishing achievement because by then he was gaunt and thin and frail and, suddenly, to those seeing him again after some while, an old man. The colour of his skin, yellow as if with jaundice, proclaimed his sad infirmity. But nothing could dim his spirit or his will-power. He knew it was his last O.C. dinner, and he was determined to enjoy it.

At the end of May, in 1979, I was many thousands of miles away, following the fortunes of England's rugby team in the Pacific island of Tonga, when I received a telephone call from my elder son, Simon, to tell me that Joe had died. I could not attend his funeral, but was touched to be asked by his family to speak at a memorial service later arranged in the Cranbrook Church of St Dunstan's and lovingly organized by his old friend Tony Congreve. 'The Cathedral of the Kentish Weald' was bursting at the seams with many generations of Old Cranbrookians gathered to honour their Mr Chips.

Here we were, I said, in a lovely old church, where a very steadfast Christian had worshipped so regularly, to salute his memory and to give thanks for the life of a great school-master. He had died after a long innings played always with the straightest of bats and after fighting his last fight, on an impossible pitch, with characteristic fortitude.

In the end, this staunch and vigorous man, sapped steadily of his strength, must have been glad to go. I suggested that the words Tennyson put into the mouth of the dying Sir Richard Grenville would have been so apposite for Joe:

> I have fought for Queen and faith
> Like a valiant man and true
> I have only done my duty
> As a man is bound to do.

Duty. My goodness, Joe did his duty for Cranbrook, and on what a scale. Another quote, from his beloved Horace, came to mind. *'Exegi monumentum aere perennius . . .'* '(My work is done:) I have built a monument more lasting than bronze.' God bless dear old Joe, and give him eternal peace and happiness in sun-kissed Elysian fields while he watches the great ones batting all day. Through those last words I battled, to no avail, against my tears.

Within a few months my old headmaster had crossed the last divide as well, at the age of eighty-one. Another host of Old Cranbrookians went back to St Dunstan's Church to honour his memory, a felicitous address being made by Sir David Muirhead, who had been my rugby captain at school and was later to become Her Majesty's Ambassador in Lima, Lisbon and Brussels. Much of what he said I have echoed or shamelessly plagiarized in this chapter.

There was some bullying of junior boys when first I went to Cranbrook but this was soon stamped out by the vigilant new headmaster. There were homosexual activities, although Cranbrook, if I can be a true judge, seemed some way in this respect from being the Sodom and Gomorrah portrayed in so many books about boys' boarding schools. Masturbation flourished, the vice-captain of the rugby XV contending in my last season that he played much better after such essential preparation.

In my latter days at school, I found myself developing an

28

affectionate regard for my fag, a good-looking young lad who, had I recognized the truth, was a substitute for the female gender. I can report with hand on heart that my interest remained platonic. I sought with unflagging zeal, though rarely much luck, to make up for lost time by orthodox pursuits in the holidays.

In declaring earlier that I had enjoyed my time at school I added that in many ways I never had it so good. Just before my fifteenth birthday I achieved some comforting School Certificate results. Two years later an equally encouraging return from the Higher Certificate papers persuaded my parents and headmaster to believe that with due diligence and the right coaching I might obtain the university scholarship in Classics which was needed for my father to contemplate sending me to Oxford or Cambridge.

I prospered on the games front too. I was in the cricket XI for five years, captaining it in the last three of them, in the rugby and hockey teams for four, being skipper of each for my last two seasons. In the clearer light of advancing years I was able to see that as a batsman I lacked the patience, concentration and temperament to aspire to much more than good club standard. I still like to suppose that my hopes on the rugby field were more firmly based, but I played my last game before I was twenty-one. For some time afterwards I could hardly bear to watch my contemporaries in action.

All round, progress at school was such that the headmaster endorsed my elevation to house captain at the age of sixteen – so I had three years in that job as well. In my last year at Cranbrook I was made head of the school and Sergeant Major in the OTC. What with that and the captaincy of cricket, rugby, hockey, fives and athletics I had become a big fish in a tiny pool.

Looking back, I do not think my revered headmaster and housemaster did me any favours at all by appointing me as captain of this or that at a relatively tender age. I began to think the world might owe me a living – and was soon to discover that it did not.

29

In a letter which Joe wrote to my father just after I had left school he observed that, 'Peter's character and temperament are of that mercurial type which must inevitably provoke storms, and it cannot honestly be said that there is anyone of any standing here whom he has not annoyed from time to time.' I dare say an arrogant eighteen-year-old deserved that stricture.

I deserved another for the way I wasted my final years at school. I had two shots at a university scholarship, failing both of them. A belief that I might have got close to an Exhibition at Oxford may have been as much inspired by vanity as the thought that I could have done the trick by working harder. I was certainly idle. It was a poor way to reward the hopes and confidence of parents and tutors.

By this time sporting horizons were long since clouded, too, my ambitions bedevilled by discomfort in the back and legs which was to become a consistently frustrating part of life. With the benefit of hindsight I would then have been less enthusiastic to opt for a military career after the Royal Military College, Sandhurst, had changed one of its rules for entry. Candidates with Higher Certificates were to be admitted without taking a written examination – provided they could pass muster in a *viva voce* test. My final year at Cranbrook went by, alas, in ever greater indolence.

In his last week *in statu pupillari* the head of the school, who ought to have been ashamed even to contemplate such an escapade, decided with one of his house prefects that they would leave their dormitory at dead of night, purloin a Morris Minor belonging to the headmaster's wife, and drive it to Hastings. Conveniently enough, those being days when security against thieves, vagabonds and hooligans was not thought necessary, the gracious lady had left her car in an unlocked garage with the ignition key still in place. Brian Kemp and I were pushing the vehicle on to the main road (hard by the local police station) when we were confronted by a third night owl, one Alan Reynolds, from another house. It seemed sensible to make a threesome of it,

30

so we all set off for Sussex by the sea. We helped ourselves to a life-belt from the beach, as evidence of target achieved, and subsequently paraded it at the end of term sing-song with the words SS *Mabel* vividly displayed around the circle. This was in honour of one of the maids in the school dining hall who, I think, had succeeded in preserving her virginity in spite of sundry efforts by my contemporaries to dispossess her of it.

The whole sorry Hastings episode came to light, I know not how, well after I had left school. It says a lot for the tolerance of my headmaster that he was prepared not only to forgive me for an act of total irresponsibility but even to joke about it. 'I hope,' he remarked, 'that you piloted my wife's car with due care and attention, and not with the reckless panache you have always associated with my own driving.'

Alan Reynolds, who was known thereafter as Peter, subsequently became an announcer on the B.B.C.'s Overseas Services. Brian Kemp was a test pilot during the war and afterwards made his fortune in property. He rang me up one day in the fifties. 'Come and have lunch at the Ritz,' he said. 'I've retired.' Having admitted to selling out for a quarter of a million pounds he became a country squire in Sussex before moving with his lovely wife, Joy, to Majorca, where sadly he died prematurely young.

Charles Wheeler, one of the most experienced and peripatetic of TV reporters, is another contemporary Old Cranbrookian to have made his mark with the B.B.C. Brian Moore, who moved from B.B.C. Radio to I.T.V., was captain of Cranbrook cricket in 1949. Yet another soccer commentator, Barry Davies, left Cranbrook early – I hasten to add for no shameful reason – in the mid-fifties. To think that of our three sports commentators only one of them has stayed loyal to the oval-shaped ball. Brian Moore was a day boy at school, soccer the winter game in his neck of the Kentish woods. Barry Davies would have been a shrewd observer of rugby for the B.B.C. if the chance had come his way. Brian's progress in his younger days was done no harm at all by an introduction I gave him to Jim Swanton. He was not the only young journalist to become an aide to the cricket guru of the *Daily Telegraph*, and profit from the experience.

School friends tend to drift apart, though if their paths should cross again the memory of an experience shared, of so much in common, enables them, briefly at least, to take up where they left off; the parting years dissolve. Even the initials, though perhaps not the surname, are remembered when you bump, twenty years on, into a face vaguely recalled from school days. 'Smithers,' its owner offers, helping you over a temporary difficulty. 'Good God, yes,' you reply triumphantly. 'Of course. J. D. G. Smithers.'

I recall one Cranbrookian from my time at school whose friendship I have treasured over the years. Tony Venniker was as idle at school as he was later to be as a medical student at St Mary's Hospital, where it took him some time to qualify as a doctor. This would never do in this supposedly enlightened age but in those days the Dean had a soft spot for anyone who could help sustain Mary's in their dominant position in Hospitals rugby.

Venniker and I started life in Crowden House in the same term and very soon were paired as half-backs in the junior colts. It became apparent to our revered housemaster, Joe, that Venniker's service at scrum-half was both lobbed and laborious, so he was soon translated into a wing forward, a position in which his outstanding mobility, ball-playing ability and instinctive sense of position brought him a fistful of tries. He was a voracious tackler too.

He would have had at least another season in the First XV if his prudent father had not removed him to a crammers' establishment to further his entry to St Mary's. His target achieved, Tony adorned the hospital's rugby team for many years, refining the abilities I have described, and also played for Middlesex, London and the Barbarians. A tolerant Dean having finally read the riot act, my old friend and muddied oaf had an able enough mind to pass his exams without difficulty – once he got down to serious work. Not long afterwards he went to South Africa, whence his father's forebears came, to acquire a practice in the North Eastern Cape. He delights to report that business was poor until he immodestly let it be known one day that he had played rugby for the Barbarians. Next morning, there was a long queue outside his surgery.

For many years now he has been in private practice in Durban where until recently he has indulged a passion for long-distance road running. My belief that he has always been something of a nut case was confirmed some time ago when we arrived to spend a holiday with Tony and his delightful young wife, Sue. We found him preparing not just for a modest marathon over twenty-six miles and a bit, but the 'Comrades' run, Durban to Pietermaritzburg (vice versa in alternate years), which is twice as long. I doff my respectful cap to anyone in his sixties fit enough and determined enough to run such a distance over highly testing terrain.

Tony ran in six 'Comrades' before giving it a rest because of mild bronchial troubles. He contents himself these days with modest half-marathons (a mere thirteen miles) at one of which I was invited in 1985 to present the awards. Ten of the first twelve runners to finish were black. Let no one suggest that road-running or athletics in South Africa are not genuinely multi-racial. Or boxing. Or football. Or cricket. The cricket authorities in the Republic have done everything within their power to meet the requirements of their counterparts elsewhere yet remain snubbed, out in the cold, on account of ever more insistent pressures from governments still prepared, hypocritically, to trade with a country whose system of apartheid almost all of us find abhorrent.

Rugby in South Africa, the game which is the Afrikaner's special pride and joy, is not yet so wholly integrated, although Dr Danie Craven, long-time president of their rugby board, has moved the most stubborn obstacles in his

ceaseless efforts to open up the game to all races regardless
of colour. I might add that rugby and cricket are not sports
in South Africa to which black people naturally turn.

Back now to sporting memories of alma mater where in
spite of aches and pains I still managed in the fifties and
sixties to play some gentle, largely ineffective cricket when
running an M.C.C. side in its annual fixture there, in our
old boys' (Lynxes) week and in county players' benefit
games.

In various fixtures at Cranbrook during that time the boys
were able to play against an impressive array of Test and
county cricketers. Denis Compton, Colin Cowdrey, Godfrey Evans, Jim Laker, 'Hopper' Levett, Jack Martin, Peter
May, Peter Richardson, Roy Swetman and Brian Valentine
were England players I lured to my old school's green and
pleasant sward. Richie Benaud captained an XI there against
Wilfred Isaacs's side from South Africa which included a
young Mike Procter and Barry Richards. Jonathan ('Pom-
Pom') Fellows-Smith was another Springbok to play there.
Arthur Phebey and Geoffrey Smith stood for Kent, Mike
Griffith for Cambridge and Sussex, Chris Winn (a former
England rugby international) for Oxford and Sussex, and
Chris Howland for Cambridge, Kent, Sussex and the
Gentlemen of England. Antony Craxton (my then TV
cricket producer), Reg Hayter (a much respected cricket
journalist), Trevor Howard, Brian Johnston and John Slater
– passionate, very useful cricketers all – served other causes.

Getting Denis Compton to play at Cranbrook I rated as
one of my better achievements. A week before the fixture I
discovered that, with his endearing inability to say 'no' to
anybody, he had pledged himself to appear in two other
games on the same day. I had to take a very firm line about
this. It stands to the great man's credit that having driven
from Buckinghamshire to Kent through the metropolis he
arrived only five minutes late.

We always played twelve-a-side in the M.C.C. fixture so
that Brian Valentine could enjoy his cigar and brandy in a

deck chair after the lunch interval. Brian, who died in 1983, epitomized all that was best in the old amateur cricketers, exuding good cheer and good companionship. Hopper Levett has been another to live life and cricket to the full, and if you have never heard him make an after-dinner speech, getting his stories mixed up, then you have missed an uproarious experience.

My old housemaster and cricket coach delighted to preside on M.C.C. match days at Cranbrook and often to stand as an umpire. But there came a time after he had retired when neither the master in charge nor his captain of cricket bothered to thank the M.C.C. manager for bringing down his team. That was not the only example of a new generation of masters taking things for granted, so I stopped going to the bother of organizing the side. I am an unrepentant old square who believes the little courtesies of life should be observed.

Things nowadays are too often taken for granted in various aspects of our social and business life. Many people seem incapable of answering letters. Those who write asking you to do them a favour rarely think to enclose a stamped addressed envelope. Then, after you have acceded to the request, they don't bother to say thank you either. A few county cricketers, prior to making a tax-free fortune in their benefit season, now conduct requests and correspondence through their business agents.

My last M.C.C. game ended in pathetic fashion. Walking forward from mid-on to pick the ball up after a batsman's defensive stroke, I collapsed in agony to the noise of something like a pistol shot, which denoted the clean rupture of an Achilles tendon. It would be nice to recall that I had been attempting something dramatic at the time.

The surgeon counselled an immediate operation, but a Test match was imminent. With some determination but less sense I took my crutches to Trent Bridge where, with acute difficulty, I mounted a perpendicular ladder to the commentary box. I subsequently went into hospital to have things stitched together again. It was after that, at another televised match, in Canterbury, when my appearance – still on crutches – was more than B.B.C. TV's head of sport in London could endure. 'Bloody hell,' I heard Bryan Cowgill exploding down the line, 'what's that stupid bugger up to now?'

On a subsequent holiday in Majorca, while his family plunged into the sea, this perspiring, plastered breadwinner cut a ridiculous figure with his posterior immersed in a rock pool and one rigid leg held aloft at forty-five degrees.

Back to Cranbrook, from which I digress. It figures prominently in these recollections not only for the memories of my time as a boy there but also because I was able later to express a lasting affection for it in practical ways. I was secretary of the Old Cranbrookians' Association for twenty-five years, my better half unstintingly doing most of the chores – as the committee and members generously acknowledged when we decided to call it a day. I am now its president.

We looked back on an era in which its old boys had done Cranbrook proud. They had subscribed to a new gymnasium and a new games pavilion bearing the name of Frank Evans. In later years they coughed up again for a new swimming pool and a major appeal for new buildings. By then the headmaster was John Kendall-Carpenter, a former England rugby captain who came from Clifton College to oversee with vision and immense dedication the most significant expansion in the school's history. By then, too, I was one of the old boys on a board of governors which concluded that the only realistic future for a school with paltry endowments lay in its wholehearted co-operation with the local education authority. With one dissentient voice the board decided that Cranbrook would become co-educational.

The transition began shortly after our two sons, Simon and Stephen, had finished their time in my old house. For part of that time, until he retired, their housemaster was the one and only Joe. With almost 750 pupils, almost half of them girls, Cranbrook in the eighties has become in some respects a very different school from the one I joined in 1932. But it still enjoys an unbroken tradition stretching back more than 400 years on the same site. It remains semi-independent in having so-called voluntary-aided status. It takes boarding and day pupils of both sexes, and it acts as the 'upper school' for a number of local establishments.

With my brief history of back trouble I was surprised to pass the medical for Sandhurst without difficulty: the doctors apparently did not think the condition deep-seated. Nine days before the war started I reported to B Company in the new building at the Royal Military College. I had been to the approved tailors in Savile Row to acquire jodhpurs and all the necessary riding kit, but Sandhurst's steeds disappeared overnight, presumably on the theory that the war would not be won by a cavalry charge. So I never got into the saddle. The so-called gentlemen cadets in a new entry were left to give their undivided attention on the parade ground to Regimental Sergeant Major ('Bosom') Brand, a fearsome man with a voice of countless decibels which could be heard in the adjoining county.

RSM Brand remained a distant though highly respected figure to cadets bashing the Sandhurst square. B Company's Sergeant-Major, a splendid Coldstreamer whose name, alas, I have forgotten, we got to know rather better. 'Chest out, Mr West, and pull that stummick in,' he adjured me once. 'You're marching like a pregnant duck.'

From my Sandhurst days as a cadet I recall no one more vividly than my platoon commander, Bernard Fergusson, of the Black Watch, an officer of brilliant, original talent whose spirited rendering of 'The Ballad of Kerriemuir', monocle affixed to one eye, was something to savour. He subsequently found fame with the Chindits under Orde Wingate in Burma and, when the war was over, acquired a knighthood and the governor-generalship of New Zealand.

In peacetime the Sandhurst course lasted for a year and a half. On ours we gained an accelerated commission in just six months, whereupon a fledgling Second Lieutenant reported for duty in Halifax at the headquarter barracks of the Duke of Wellington's (West Riding) Regiment, 33rd of Foot. The Duke's had the reputation of being the best rugby regiment in the Army – which seemed substantiated by the presence in Halifax of Jeffrey Reynolds (England and British Lions) and Charlie Grieve (Scotland). Ken Jackson (Scotland) and Freddie Huskisson (England) were two more international players who joined the Duke's at about this time.

The winter of 1939–40 was a harsh one. Wellesley Barracks, a thousand feet up in the Pennines, seemed a rugged place to an effete southerner accustomed to milder climates. It did not seem a lot warmer when I was posted to the 10th Battalion at Wentworth Woodhouse, near Rotherham, where the Officers' Mess was installed in Earl Fitzwilliam's old quarters and his Lordship came regularly for a stiffener at lunch time on the Sabbath.

From there we moved to the east coast of Yorkshire, near Bridlington, where we awaited Adolf's projected invasion with precious little to repulse it if the worst should befall us. I fell into the bad books of my company commander when he turned up one day to find me playing cards with my platoon NCOs. This was not approved behaviour for an officer and gentleman seeking to retain the respect of his troops. Soon afterwards I was despatched to a special job with the Brigadier at his headquarters. I concluded that my battalion CO and company commander had thought this the best way of getting rid of an undisciplined subaltern. I am not ashamed to say that I wept when I said goodbye to the loyal West Riding lads who had served in my platoon on the east coast. For my money, they were the salt of this earth.

In the summer of 1941 I was posted back to Sandhurst as an instructor of officer cadets. It seemed strange, two years into the war, that the authorities could not have found someone who had seen a shot fired in anger. At the end of a year I took the chance of going on a Commando course at Lochailort, on the Road to the Isles. A tough but stimulating three weeks in the Highlands left me wishing that I had been able to enjoy them in prime condition. I was in miserable physical shape when reporting back to the 1st battalion of the Duke's, then stationed in Norfolk.

Shortly afterwards I entered a local hospital where I remained on my back while the Battalion sailed to join the 2nd Army in North Africa. Sustaining heavy losses, the Duke's fought their way through Algeria, Tunis, Sicily and Italy. Apart from a posting to a training camp near Chester, the end of Captain West's thoroughly undistinguished war was spent in the orthopaedic wards of sundry hospitals. A final diagnosis, spondylitis (an arthritic condition of the spine), seemed a far cry from the fibrositis first suspected at school. The cure, it seemed, could not be found. I was invalided out of the Army in 1944.

'What did you do in the war, Daddy?'

'Alas, my son, nothing to make me feel a hero.'

What now to do for a living? I had no degree, no professional qualifications. I might yet have managed to obtain a grant towards a university place but lacked the mental resilience to settle for several years of study. I knew, too, that in another area of my life even the milder athletic activities would have to be pursued at half-cock.

My first job was as assistant to the Controller of the Soldiers', Sailors' and Airmen's Families Association (known as SSAFA for short). It was to end ignominiously but there were two unlooked-for bonuses. One of these was to find myself working with Alison Barnes, a vibrant soul and an experienced free-lance journalist who was in charge of SSAFA's press activities. She taught me some essential rudiments of her trade and encouraged me to believe that I might consider a different way to earn a living.

The ignominy occurred as a result of my clashing swords with SSAFA's chairman, an elderly Air-Vice-Marshal. I cannot now recall the details of our disagreement but I thought him pompous and stupid, and the feeling was clearly mutual. It does not do for impulsive young men to argue with the boss. I was sacked. But I more than got my own back with bonus number two.

The Controller's secretary at SSAFA was a slim, extremely attractive girl called Pauline to whom I had taken a distinct if distant fancy without ever getting the slightest indication that my interest was reciprocated. A few weeks after I had been sent packing by the Air-Vice-Marshal, a letter to Pauline produced a more encouraging response. Her social diary happened to be blank at the time and, yes, she would be agreeable to meeting me in the old Oddenino's at the bottom of Regent Street. I primed her with gin and orange at prices I could not really afford and proceeded during a blossoming association to encourage her taste for beer and cheap Chinese meals. One thing led to another. Peter and Paul were joined together in holy matrimony in September 1946.

Paul's father had died when she was only five. Her mother then left her to be brought up by a devoted aunt who must have wondered on our wedding day whether she had been wise to surrender her niece to an impecunious young journalist. I had been accepted by the Exchange Telegraph Agency for a trial period of three months at five guineas a week, and given assurance that if I made the grade, my salary would then be raised to nine guineas (then the minimum union rate in London). With such riches in those days I could aspire to keep a wife in wedded bliss, if not in the comfort to which she had been accustomed.

Nine guineas a week was certainly no passport to a penthouse. We despaired of finding a flat within my resources but eventually solved the problem through the personal column of *The Times*. 'Young ex-Regular Officer's marriage postponed till find small self-contained FLAT/HOUSE, preferably S London outskirts: rent not exceeding £3 weekly: can anyone help?' It worked. An elderly lady

offered us a basement flat in her Edwardian manse at Weybridge. It was close enough to the station to convey an
impression that we would be living on Platform 4.

There were two special clauses in the agreement which
required to be observed. There must be no babies in the
West menage, and would we please be careful not to use the
toilet – or at least to pull the chain – after 11 o'clock at night?
The landlady's bedroom was immediately above it, and the
plumbing made disturbing sounds.

There was no mention at that stage of a coke boiler which
in anything like a northerly wind emitted its fumes directly
into the kitchen (there was no dearth of icy blasts at the end
of the winter of 1946–7). In a bitter spell of weather lasting
from mid-January to early March even our main water
supply was frozen solid. These were two little trials in early
married life. A third was the night duty roster to which I
was seconded at Exchange Telegraph, sub-editing Reuter's
reports of England's first cricket tour of Australia in the
post-war years. Another was the painful deterioration of a
wonky back which the attention of doctors, osteopaths and
even a faith healer in Cornwall had done nothing to
improve.

Depressed and difficult to live with, I sought the advice
and help of Mr Michael Kremer, a leading orthopaedic
surgeon who had treated me at a war-time hospital in
Oxford. Praise be, the course of deep X-rays he prescribed
reduced the pain and stopped things getting worse. Of
those who have helped to shape my life I owe no greater
thanks than to him.

Chapter Two

—————————————

At Taunton early in 1947 a legendary figure from cricket's Golden Age brought his Corinthian presence to the press box on behalf of the *Sunday Graphic*, long since defunct. When a young reporter found himself sitting next to C. B. Fry it seemed akin to being at God's right hand.

I knew the essential facts about his remarkably varied life. Fry and Ranjitsinhji, bestriding the batting stage. Cricket for England. Association football for England. A share in the world's long jump record. A fourth Blue, for rugby, denied him only through injury. Top entry scholar at Wadham College, Oxford where he acquired a First Degree in Classics, and men of the calibre of F. E. Smith (Lord Birkenhead) and John Simon – both of them to become leading Ministers of the Crown – played second or third fiddle. At Wadham, as the saying went, it was Fry and small fry.

In his recent biography, *C.B.*, Clive Ellis observes that for sheer versatility Charles Burgess Fry was unique. 'In one man there was a scholar, poet, novelist, journalist, editor, teacher, politician, cricketer, soccer player, rugby player, golfer, angler, athlete, skater, skier, sculler, diver, tennis player, hunter and boxer.' He alludes later to his prowess on the dance floor, and confirms that at the League of Nations in the twenties he was tentatively invited to become King of Albania.

It happened, one Saturday in Taunton, that a telephonist

43

hired to convey Fry's account of the proceedings to London failed to put in an appearance. I averted a possible crisis with the sycophantic suggestion that it would be an honour for me to do the job myself. The offer was cordially accepted.

C. B. Fry must have thought I accomplished the task with some panache because he said afterwards: 'Have you ever thought, my boy, of becoming a B.B.C. commentator?' I replied with honesty that I had not, though admitting abject failure, some while earlier, to pass a test as a radio newsreader. 'I shall send your name,' Fry announced, 'to the Head of Outside Broadcasts.'

I am ashamed to admit that I scarcely believed him. I was not then aware that, presiding over the training ship *Mercury* on the Hamble river near Portsmouth, he had spent much of his life giving young men a push up the ladder. Within a week he had sent a letter which wished me well and indicated that I should telephone the head man's secretary at the B.B.C. The Head of Outside Broadcasts (HOB to use one of the Corporation's myriad abbreviations) was then S. J. de Lotbiniere, known to one and all as 'Lobby': a man of lofty stature endowed with a most genial nature and a clear, incisive, cultured mind which analyzed the content and delivery of a broadcast with the surest touch.

Lobby was generous enough to give me half an hour of his valuable time during which he expounded a masterful treatise on the art of commentary and explained that while many aspirants may have thought they had a natural calling, few indeed were chosen. But he added that this was a time of expansion for his department in the post-war years. I should go away and practise and then, if I could advance a convincing case, he might arrange for me to do a recorded test commentary at a county match.

How could I practise in public without being thought by near neighbours to be deranged? The idea at first seemed mildly daft. Then it occurred to me that there were plenty of spots at a county game where one could soliloquize in relative peace. On more congested occasions I 'thought' through a commentary without uttering a sound.

I am inclined to believe now that the only meaningful way a commentator can improve his skills is at the public's suffering expense. But emboldened then by preparation, however inadequate, and fired by a growing enthusiasm for what seemed the perfect way to earn a crust, I sought further audience with Lobby. Bless him, it got me to base camp two.

Soon afterwards there came a call from Rex Alston, for many years the B.B.C.'s senior radio commentator on cricket, rugby and athletics. He is eighty-five now, marvellously well preserved and still contributing cricket and rugby reports for the *Daily* and *Sunday Telegraph*. His many admirers were greatly relieved to be informed that following his obituary notice printed in *The Times* in October 1985, the report of his demise, as in the case of Mark Twain, was greatly exaggerated.

'Young West,' Rex announced on the telephone in 1947. 'We are going to give you a commentary test at Lord's.' So to that hallowed sanctuary, in trepidation and due course, I was summoned to record a period of commentary. But alas, in a golden summer when the illustrious duo of Denis Compton and Bill Edrich plundered well over 7,000 runs between them, this was one of the rare occasions when it rained. 'Never mind,' Rex said, 'just talk away for five minutes about the weather, the sides, the prospects and anything else that comes to mind.' I am sorry to say that not a lot did.

I have always envied those confident, self-assured mortals who sit in front of a microphone for the first time as if to the manner born. Taut with nerves, unable to be in relaxed command of the breathing system, I managed three or four minutes of rather incoherent comment. 'Not too bad,' Rex observed with that encouraging air which in his school-mastering days must have marked his attitude to unpromising pupils. 'We'll have you back again when there's some actual play to talk about.'

Back I went, a few days later, to a cramped commentary

box situated at that time above the Middlesex and England dressing room. My nervous disorders were still too obviously apparent. I experienced distinct difficulty in maintaining an interesting flow when fast bowlers delivered seemingly interminable overs. But I may have done a bit better when describing the essential action. 'Not too bad,' Rex adjudicated yet again, without actually adding, 'Don't call us. We'll call you.'

Convinced that I had muffed my lines and hearing not a word from the B.B.C. for six weeks, I had abandoned all hopes of a utopian future when Rex Alston came on the line again. 'We're a commentator short for the Warwickshire–South African match,' he declared. 'We're throwing you to the lions.'

To Edgbaston, then, young Daniel journeyed for his first outside broadcast, mindful of his luck in being given a chance when the Corporation was looking for new voices and at a time, moreover, when a performer could indulge himself for half hour periods at a stretch. That era is long since gone. Nowadays anyone covering a county match on Radio 2 is fortunate to get more than a few minutes to himself. Would-be commentators are better advised to learn their trade with local or hospital radio, and move on from there.

In the early post-war years, before the profits from a football pool and the good commercial sense of the Supporters' Club as well as the Warwickshire administration had begun to transform Edgbaston into an impressive arena for cricket, there were no commentary boxes, for radio or TV, sited with a view behind the bowler's arm. In 1947 the radio broadcasts were made from a hen-coop of a room into which yours truly and his B.B.C. Midlands producer, James Pestridge, were fitted with some difficulty. It would never have done for Jimmy Pestridge now – he boasts a generous girth – nor at any time for Jim Swanton, whose substantial poundage I was happy to see acting as ballast whenever, in later years, the TV scaffolding rocked alarmingly in high winds.

Another drawback for a tyro commentator at Edgbaston in 1947 was the proximity of the visiting team's balcony, which enabled the touring South Africans to hear what was being said. It would not worry me now. In a similar situation I would have the confidence to say what I thought and to feel that players could like it or lump it. But I had no such confidence then. What right, I asked myself, had a new boy to speak with pretended authority about famous men such as Alan Melville, Dudley Nourse, Bruce Mitchell and all? From time to time I was conscious of backward glances, of disbelief or a slight distaste, rather as if there was a curious smell on the landing.

On a happier note, the broadcast schedule provided for most of my efforts to be directed exclusively towards the overseas service, which meant that very few of my friends were able to hear them. When I was heard, mercifully briefly, on parochial transmissions, my wife was so excited she rushed upstairs from our basement flat in Weybridge to tell our landlady, not without due pride, that *her husband was on the air*. 'Where's he flying to?' was the octogenarian's incredulous response.

Peter Cranmer, the Warwickshire captain and an England centre threequarter of distinction in the thirties, may be delighted to know that the one clear memory I retain of that cricket match is his buccaneering hundred made in only ninety minutes. I see from *Wisden*, which at one old London bookshop used to be found under 'Religions' rather than 'Sports and Pastimes', that Dudley Nourse made a double hundred. Yet Cranmer's century made for the liveliest commentary, and I was grateful for his help. These days, his mobility is considerably restricted by what he calls 'one stroke too many', but he bears up with characteristic courage and good cheer.

In 1948 I began modestly to spread my commentator's wings. Nicholas Crocker, then senior Outside Broadcasts producer in Bristol and later to make a notable mark with the Natural History unit, invited me to cover several county derbies for the West region and, thanks to Rex Alston, I even had the pleasure of doing duty at a Kent match in Canterbury. The England wicketkeeper and batsman, Les Ames, who had been foremost amongst my schoolboy heroes, was not behind the stumps that day but stationed in the deep field, just under the commentary box. Once again, I asked myself, how could I justify this new relationship between a great player and one who as a callow schoolboy had acquired his autograph on the old Angel ground in Tonbridge almost twenty years before?

As well as pushing a young pretender into likely avenues for advancement C. B. Fry invited me to his private box at Lord's where, surrounded by luminaries of the arts such as Clifford Bax, Edmund Blunden, James Agate and Sir John Squire, he would, between the declamation and translation of Greek elegiacs, demonstrate with his gold-topped cane how batsmen then on view might overcome their inadequacies. He bade me welcome to lunch at his club in Mayfair, leaping up the stairs four steps at a time, even at the age of seventy-six, and I am reminded of a tale about his athletic prowess – I think apocryphal – in the then *Manchester Guardian*.

'C. B. Fry,' the writer observed, 'could, in his prime, jump backwards on to a mantelpiece from a standing start.' Much joy was caused amongst readers of the early edition in which the first two letters of his intended last word were substituted by an 'f'. Strange, sometimes absurd or disastrous things can occur to the telephoned message via copytaker, sub-editors' desk and eventual print, as all journalists know too well. On this occasion the unfortunate error was spotted in time for a correction in later editions. Second time round, the *M.G.* did not do much better. The 'f' was changed to a 't'.

Most of my formative years were spent in Kent to which county in cricketing terms I owe undying allegiance. But it was in the West Country that my feet were planted firmly on a broadcasting road, and I shall always retain affectionate memories of the Somerset, Gloucestershire and Hampshire teams in those days. Moreover, the press boxes in those counties were often illumined by the presence of R. C. ('Crusoe') Robertson-Glasgow, erstwhile of Oxford University and Somerset, whose memories and effervescent humour were a source of unending delight. Surely no one wrote about the game of cricket with greater charm or more consistent wit.

In the Somerset side of the early post-war era the old firm of Wellard and Andrews still shared the new ball. Bertie Buse swung it prodigiously in helpful conditions at military medium, and contrived to look cheerful when his benefit match finished in one day. The rotund Horace Hazell wheeled away, slow left arm, with persistent, metronomic accuracy. An up-and-coming all rounder, Maurice Tremlett, who died prematurely young in 1984, bowled fast and effectively enough to earn himself two tours with M.C.C. overseas.

Arthur Wellard hit sixes into the River Tone almost as often as he had done before the war, though not always as straight. Bill Andrews, still happily preserved, retains one claim to local notoriety which cannot be challenged: as player or committee man he has been sacked by the county on four different occasions.

A lovely man, William Andrews; entirely without malice but often capable of putting his feet (size twelve) well and truly in it. I could even forgive him for twice bowling out Les Ames for a pair. In the late seventies, at Clarence Park in Weston-Super-Mare, he gave me one of the funniest interviews I have ever conducted on television. He recalled how Somerset had engaged him, in 1930, on a £10 a match basis, the player paying his own hotel bills at away games; how in those days amateur bowlers always seemed to get preference when the opposition's tail enders batted; how he once took 8 for 12 against Surrey at the Oval, achieving a hat-trick with the last ball of one over and the first two of the next, without being aware of the distinction until the umpire told him; how he and three fellow pros, finding B & B at about four bob a head in a London boarding house, had to make do in one single and one double bed.

Harold Gimblett, as a man in prime batting form, was given the single. Andrews, Hazell and one other shared the double. Hazell's substantial presence left little room for anyone else. A restless night for the trio was not improved by Gimblett going 'walkabout' as dawn came up, complaining that he was making too many runs and couldn't sleep.

In similar if rather less congested circumstances Wellard and Andrews often shared a double bed on their cricketing travels. This apparently worked out well enough except for the night when Bill was woken up with what felt like a knife in his back. The knife turned out to be Arthur's dentures, which had come adrift.

Bill Andrews eventually got round to airing these and other reminiscences in a book written in collaboration with David Foot. I am pleased to report that my suggestion for its title was adopted: *The Hand That Bowled Bradman*. Not too many bowlers could claim such distinction. Bill achieved the feat at Taunton in 1938 when Bradman had made 202.

When I watched the Indians play at Taunton in 1946, their opening batsman, Vijay Merchant, had made a great many cultured runs and was clearly a prime target for Somerset's attack. On a morning made for swing bowlers the visitors were shot out for 64, Andrews and Buse sharing all the wickets at a modest cost. Half the side was out for a pittance when Andrews enquired of a colleague: 'When's this geezer Merchant coming in?'

'You had him caught behind by Wally Luckes in the first over,' came the reply.

In those days, as had long been the case before the Second World War, amateurs in what their paid colleagues termed 'fancy hats' often kept professionals out of county sides, especially during the school holidays. This certainly was not the case with M. M. Walford, a most gifted all-round athlete

50

who but for Hitler's intervention would surely have added a full England rugby cap to those he won in wartime as a centre threequarter. Nor could it have applied to another Somerset amateur and subsequent captain, R. J. O. Meyer, a forceful, distinctly original leader who once was so enraged by what Tom Goddard had been able to achieve for Gloucestershire on a helpful Bristol pitch that he made a point of likening it, publicly, to the beach at Weston-super-Mare.

Of Somerset's premier batsman, who was to take his own life in 1978, the whole sad and arresting tale has been told by David Foot in his book, *Harold Gimblett*. Sub-titled *Tormented Genius of Cricket*, it is a riveting cricket biography. Suffice it for me to remember Gimblett's halcyon days, the thunderous innings he played – and how I wish I had seen the one a lad from the Quantocks made, in a mere sixty-three minutes, in his first innings for the county, against Essex at Frome in 1935! A century, as David Foot has recalled, that belonged to fiction. It made Gimblett a sporting celebrity overnight. Yet he loathed the spotlight.

I was lucky to witness a goodly number of Gimblett's hundreds after the war, none of them more memorable than one he fashioned against Kent on a dusting turner of a pitch at Gravesend. Quite simply, he put Kent's bowling to the sword. That Kentish attack included the England leg-spinner, Doug Wright, who could be a formidable opponent on a bland surface, let alone when bounce and turn were his allies. It was one of the most thrilling innings I have seen – akin to a superb hundred I saw Denis Compton make for Middlesex, against Kent and Wright again, on a helpful pitch at Lord's.

In spite of his glowing deeds for Somerset on either side of the war, Harold Gimblett played in only three Test matches for England – twice against India in 1936 and once against the West Indies three summers later. He opened the innings for his country in the unofficial 'Victory Test' at the war's end; in 1950 he was summoned to Trent Bridge for the third Test against the West Indies. But arriving there with a carbuncle on his neck, he was not chosen to play. Was he haunted by self-doubt, by his almost obsessive disregard for most selectors and committee men? He never suffered fools gladly. He could be blunt to the point of extreme tactlessness. He scorned an M.C.C. hierarchy at Lord's which denied an England player entry to the pavilion unless he could find a member to sign him in.

But he possessed an impish sense of humour. At Taunton one morning, when about to launch a Somerset innings, he asked me what time I would be on the air. 'Twelve to twelve thirty,' I naively replied. 'Then I'll make things difficult for you,' he rather ominously replied.

By midday he was in the forties and his partner, Frank Lee, happily conceding the strike, had made about half a dozen. But once having noted that the broadcast had begun, Harold, between noon and half past twelve, pushed the first five balls of every over directly to a close fielder (or offered no stroke at all), took a single off the last and clearly enjoyed himself as he observed the commentator struggling to sustain a lively account when there was precious little activity to get excited about. Then in the next half hour, my commentary stint completed, he made another forty or so.

More than any other West Country man Gimblett left a lasting impression on the memory of a young broadcaster. What dazzling impact might he have made in one-day cricket? That question might be asked, I concede, about many great batsmen of earlier eras. What price would England have paid more recently for a fit and willing Gimblett to open their innings in a less exalted era? Yet selectors, over the years, have often failed to stand consistently by the out-and-out aggressors. This caution extends to other sports, notably rugby union, when a back capable of winning a match by his outstanding virtues in attack has been ruled out on account of his fallibility, real or imagined, in defence.

Jim Laker tells me of an unofficial Test between a

Commonwealth XI and India in Bombay in 1950 when the touring side needed only 49 for victory in the last innings. 'Dattu Phadkar, who was no slouch, opened to Gimblett with a Carmody field – just two in front and everyone else up close. Dear old Harold plonked the first ball straight over the sightscreen for 6.' James also likes it to be known that he had 5 for 88 in the second innings off (his italics) *65 overs*.

In his approach to batting, Charles Barnett, the Gloucestershire opener, had a great deal in common with Gimblett. At Trent Bridge against Australia in 1938, he once needed one ball after lunch to complete a hundred on the first day of a Test match. This sort of performance makes things a lot easier for his colleagues – as was amply proved when Len Hutton, Eddie Paynter (a not out double 'ton') and Denis Compton also made hundreds in the same England innings.

Charlie Barnett, who was known as 'the Governor', for a long time managed to avoid making two noughts in the same match. There came an occasion at Swansea when, having failed to trouble the scorers in the first innings, he hit the first ball of the second straight out of the ground on to the beach. 'I haven't bagged a pair yet,' the Governor announced to anyone within earshot, 'and I don't intend to start now.'

By 1948, when an elegant, upstanding young batsman by the name of Tom Graveney was establishing himself in the Gloucestershire side, Charles Barnett opened their innings with George Emmett, a player of genuine class and culture who had the misfortune to be chosen for his only Test match when Ray Lindwall and Keith Miller were at their peak, not to mention that gangling left-arm bowler, Bill Johnston. It was on a greenish pitch, too.

Emmett got his chance with England at Old Trafford when, following the previous encounter at Lord's, Len Hutton was dropped – an omission which caused no end of a stir, not least in the Dales. Another Gloucestershire batsman, the trustworthy left hander, Jack Crapp, was also given his first Test cap in Manchester and survived for the next one, at Headingley, where his luck temporarily ran out.

At Old Trafford, but for a nasty turn in the weather, England might well have notched their one victory in the series. Denis Compton had made a brave, resounding hundred after nicking a bouncer from Lindwall on to his forehead. At Headingley, where 1,723 runs were scored in a record aggregate for a match in England, Australia took the rubber and set another record by making 404 for 3 wickets (Arthur Morris 182, Bradman 173 not out) in the last innings.

With only one specialist spin bowler, Jim Laker, on a pitch then taking a generous amount of turn, the England captain, Norman Yardley, resorted to the unorthodox arts of Compton, who got Lindsay Hassett out. But a mixture of left-arm leg breaks and 'chinamen' were dispatched for 82 runs in 15 overs, while four more overs of right arm leg breaks from Len Hutton went for 30. A great wicketkeeper, Godfrey Evans, suffering a bad day, missed two stumpings and finished the match very close to tears. Crapp, at slip, put down two of the three catches missed by England.

I touch upon this English disaster if only to include a tale to which I have always been addicted. The home side was based in Leeds at the Queen's Hotel where the receptionist, a young lady to whom the noble game was something of a mystery, booked in the England players. She had heard in the vaguest fashion about illustrious figures such as Hutton, Compton and Bedser.

The first two of these had booked in when the Gloucestershire representative arrived in the foyer. Seeking to advertise her expertise, she said brightly: 'Good afternoon, sir. Bedser?' 'No, Crapp,' came the rejoinder. 'Second door on the left,' the receptionist advised.

Another Gloucestershire story may bear re-telling since it illustrates the genius of Wally Hammond and the genuine awe with which he was regarded by his colleagues. In a summer when Tom Goddard finished with a haul of 248 first-class wickets, 15 of them were acquired against Kent on a spiteful, dusting surface at Bristol. That lean and hungry off-spinner preened himself in the dressing room after Kent had been bowled to defeat. But Hammond poured scorn on the quality of Kent's batting, suggesting that he could have played Goddard – even on that pitch – with the proverbial stick of rhubarb. Kent's team had departed for their next engagement when the Gloucestershire side once more took up their fielding positions. Goddard bowled. Without hint of an error Hammond faced him using only the *edge* of his bat.

In Hampshire, where Desmond Eagar first as captain and then as secretary carried the flag so selflessly until his premature death, this young commentator seemed always assured of a welcome. I cannot speak for the atmosphere in Hampshire's dressing room in the days of Lord Tennyson, George Brown and Philip Mead, but when I first came to know its occupants in 1946, it had an air of genuine friendliness which has long persisted.

Johnny Arnold, one of the few men to be capped by England at cricket and soccer, Lofty Herman, later a first-class umpire, and Neil McCorkell were nearing the end of their careers. Charles Knott, an off-spinner good enough to play for the Gentlemen, was making a notable mark. Jim Bailey, ruddy of complexion, ever cheerful, accumulated runs and wickets. Leo Harrison was preparing to take over as wicketkeeper from McCorkell. In 1949 a 25-year-old bowler, Derek Shackleton, took 100 wickets in his first season and, it may be surprising now to relate, was only 86 runs short of the 'double'.

I liked Jim Bailey's tale of his former skipper, Lord Tennyson, who was batting at Old Trafford one day when the nightwatchman, Lofty Herman, came out to join him in sepulchral light. Arriving at the crease with a gloved hand cupped to one ear, Lofty said: 'I'll be able to hear you, my Lord, but where the hell are you?' On another occasion Jim Bailey's wild throw missed the stumps by a wide margin, hit his captain on the shin and laid him prostrate for several minutes. Staggering to his feet again, Lord Tennyson said: 'Bailey, you're useless. Leave the field.' 'But I can't go, my Lord,' Jim replied. 'I'm bowling, and the over isn't finished yet.'

Chapter Three

AFTER A ONE-NIGHT stint on the panel of 'What's My Line?' in 1953 I was offered the chair of a new panel game called 'Why?' when Roy Plomley was indisposed. This was based on the idea that a panel of four people – initially Pat Burke, Brenda Bruce, Richard Attenborough and W. J. Brown, a former independent MP – should alternate as parents and children, the latter posing those awkward or impossible questions which can be the despair of their elders. A jury of four genuine parents pronounced their verdict.

Having viewed the first programme and predicted in the *Daily Telegraph* a long life for it, L. Marsland Gander seemed to find himself in a minority of one. The B.B.C.'s switchboard at Lime Grove was swamped with angry protests from the public – to an extent hitherto unprecedented when a new programme made its bow. As summer stand-in for the immensely popular 'What's My Line?' it was generally regarded as a total flop. 'Nothing,' Dr Johnson had remarked several centuries ago, 'is more hopeless than a scheme of merriment.' The boss of B.B.C. Television, then Cecil McGivern, responded to the pressure of critics and public, and took it off the air after two more programmes. He was thoughtful enough to send me a personal letter of commiseration.

'Why?' having so swiftly expired, the B.B.C. at once came up with yet another panel game called 'Guess My Story?'

and invited me as chairman – after Gilbert Harding had failed a test recording – to do the honours again. It was produced by Brian Tesler, a television whizz-kid of brilliant talent who, soon after the B.B.C. lost its monopoly in 1956, was snapped up by I.T.V. He is now chairman and managing director of London Weekend Television.

'Guess My Story?' featured challengers who had figured in the recent news. One of them was a Cambridge undergraduate, Jonathan Miller by name. A panel comprising the actresses Helen Cherry and Joan Heal, the actor Jack Watling and the author-broadcaster Michael Pertwee had to unravel what their story was. This new game had a degree of audience participation which 'Why?' had altogether lacked. It was generally liked by the viewers and the professional pundits. 'Panel and chairmen were as good as could be expected,' Peter Black wrote in the *Daily Mail*, 'when you reflect that they had been sitting around for seventeen minutes waiting for Glynebourne to finish.' Very few programmes were recorded in those days. The *radio* (my italics) critic of the *Manchester Guardian* suggested that Peter West could conduct the game just as well if he gave his smile an occasional rest. But 1953 had some good memories for me. I came second to Benny Hill in a *News Chronicle* poll for the new TV personality of the year. Sir Mortimer Wheeler was third.

'Guess My Story?' ran for three series, eventually succeeding 'What's My Line?' in the Sunday evening peak viewing slot when Eamonn Andrews and company took a rest. After its first run Brian Tesler was elevated to oversee all panel games, Dickie Leeman took over the production and the actress Eunice Gayson was a panellist with a big following. For its third and last outing a distinguished young athlete called Chris Chataway, who not long before had beaten the Czech, Vladimir Kutz, in a classic duel over 5,000 metres at the White City, was invited to join the panel but decided instead to make his name on television in programmes more intellectually demanding.

The last thing 'Guess My Story?' needed was a national newspaper strike, but it now got one. That was no help to our cause. By the end of that series, anyway, the public was getting bored by a proliferation of panel games. Thinking itself on to a good thing, the B.B.C. had been busy flogging a willing horse to death.

About this time I was invited by the *Daily Telegraph* to chair their food and cookery brains trust with a panel which included Lady Isobel Barnett (by now elegantly established on 'What's My Line?'), Constance Spry and Fanny and Johnnie Cradock. The formidable Fanny had no difficulty in dominating the proceedings as well as the wretched head waiters who failed to come up to scratch in the hotels we patronized. Many years later my wife and I were invited to help celebrate Johnnie's sixtieth birthday at a mouth-watering buffet in their Blackheath garden and, some time after that, to dine in exalted company around a beautiful marble-topped table covered by a pale blue organza cloth. A sumptuous meal, superbly cooked by Fanny, was served by young men wearing white gloves. There were no condiments on the table. My wife confessed afterwards to some anxiety lest her husband should qualify for a Bateman cartoon by asking for the salt.

The head cook and bottle washer in our modest household displayed further anxiety symptoms when we thought it time to return the compliment. What tasty dish to set before a queen? It really did not matter, as things turned out. Fanny, feeling poorly, never touched a thing. This did not deter her from holding court for the entire evening. When Johnnie was able to get a word in he confessed *inter alia* to having played rugby with Victor Silvester. He and Victor at once went even higher in my estimation.

By then even 'What's My Line?' had come to the end of its B.B.C. road: the sagger maker's bottom knocker and 887 other challengers had invited the panel to unravel their line of business. At least we went out with a bang on 'Guess My Story?' when the Crazy Gang brought the ceiling down –

plaster, flour and all – on the heads of the four panellists. Eunice Gayson and Elizabeth Allan were not best pleased. Nor was Peter Black in the *Daily Mail*. Of panel games as a whole he wrote that they had become second division television. Of this particular chairman, whom he found to be quite out of his depth, he observed: 'I wish people who have earned one reputation would not gamble with it by trying to earn another.' He may well have been right, but a reputation, alas, does not pay the bills.

The demise of 'Guess My Story?' and the vogue for panel games did not quite spell the end of my links with television's world of light entertainment. I was invited to appear on shows with Fred Emney and Terry Thomas, which I think did me no harm, and also with Dave King, which almost certainly did. A role as Dave King's stooge, subjected to several indignities I should have had the sense to decline, brought letters from viewers, kindly disposed, who implored me to stick to my original sporting last. Participation with Dave King in a song and dance routine, 'The Waiter, The Porter, and the Upstairs Maid', was a relatively harmless exercise, it is true. With no voice and little more sense of rhythm I drove a patient producer, Ernest Maxin, to near despair.

As a free-lance under no contract to the B.B.C., I still needed to perceive on which side my bread was buttered but was not inhibited from participating in the television commercials now being screened on the independent channel. These produced such a healthy addition to my income that I was tempted to think they might be the lazy man's open sesame to a life of slippered ease. Yet I am glad, on reflection, that my manager turned down an offer from one of the detergent giants for a sum comfortably in excess of my entire annual income from the Beeb.

I remembered doing one commercial for a well-known brand of coffee which, thanks to a press campaign which ran in harness with it, had me dubbed by Spanish waiters at a Majorcan hotel as Señor Nescafé. I made another, for Gillette, with the racing driver, Mike Hawthorn, who drove me round the Silverstone track for an experience I won't soon forget, and then flew me back to Surrey in his own aircraft. Shortly afterwards he was killed in an accident on the A3.

Yet another ad for Gillette featured the Welsh boxer, Dai Dower, just before he flew off to South America to fight for the world flyweight title. No expense was spared. The commercial would be shown just as soon as the new champion was crowned. But, alas, it never reached our screens. Dai Dower was knocked out in round one.

For the British School of Motoring I made thirteen *live* sixty-second spots featuring drivers who had just passed their tests: an exercise unthinkable in these days and fraught with manifold problems. 'The most ambitious live commercial campaign yet seen on television,' a trade critic wrote. Ambitious indeed. But it worked.

For the new Vauxhall Viva, Katie Boyle and I chalked up another 'first': a commercial which lasted for *six* minutes. For a canned vegetable I made one which drew this reaction from a dissatisfied viewer: 'Why don't you stick to Bird's Eye peas? They're full of wind as well.'

About this time I also put a tentative toe into the purified waters of fashion shows. This was thanks yet again to Eamonn Andrews, who was unable to compere an up-market affair at the Dorchester. Not understanding half the technical jargon in the script provided, I shamelessly borrowed some Bob Hope jokes and interspersed my rendering with a few off-the-cuff remarks not all of which were well received by the leading mannequin of the day. 'This,' I said of one shimmering creation she exhibited, 'will cost you five hundred guineas . . . empty.' It may not have been original, but it got a laugh from the audience – and a killing look from the catwalk.

Emboldened by this modest success, I embroidered the piece when hired to introduce further big shows. These included the Fabric and Fashion Fair at the Festival Hall, the British Nylon and Men's Trade Fairs at the Royal Albert

Hall, and the Jewellery Fair also chez Albert. I defy anybody to suggest that five shows a day in a hot and debilitating atmosphere is not hard and repetitive work. It seemed to me that some lighthearted relief was called for. Trade audiences – far harder to please than the general public on these occasions – seemed to enjoy it.

By then I had made up my mind that I was going to play the script my way or not at all. But this, of course, was at a time when fashion shows were being dragged out of a stilted, conventional past into an era when they would be projected with a showman's flair. I was dispatched for a week in Toronto to front just such a performance at the British Trade Fair. The Canadians seemed impressed to observe the Brits letting their hair down.

It was rewarding, beyond the field of outside broadcasts, to be asked from time to time to get my teeth into serious programmes. One such was 'First Hand', thoughtfully produced by Paul Johnstone and Nancy Thomas, which recalled historic events through the eyes of those who had witnessed them. It covered the first flight across the Atlantic, by Alcock and Brown; the sinking of the Titanic; women's suffrage; Shackleton's expedition to the Antarctic; tanks in the First World War; and the reign of King Edward VIII.

Another was 'First Years at Work', a series for school leavers offering guidance in the choice of careers. It was practical, down-to-earth fare and I thoroughly enjoyed every minute of it as it ran for the best part of a dozen years. Peter Scroggs, Peter Montagnon and Gordon Croton were its successive producers: professionals all and a joy to work with.

In radio, I did several stints on the old 'Housewives' Choice' programme in the days when disc jockeys composed their own programme of records and were thus besieged by the song pluggers of Denmark Street in efforts to get their latest masterpieces – or monstrosities – on the air. I resolved the problem by playing most of them, which seemed fair to one and all.

I hold to the view that for anyone with a relaxed manner in

front of a microphone and a modest line in patter the job of a
disc jockey is an easy, agreeable way to knock up a living. A
very few, such as Terry Wogan, elevate it to an art form.
Another, of course, is Jimmy Young, who for many years has
sustained his performance with a zestful professionalism to
be admired. He has become one of the best interviewers in
the business. Jimmy, a former pop idol, was just embarking
on his new career as a disc jockey when, somewhat to my
surprise, I was asked to host some shows for Radio Luxem-
bourg. Another person looking for pastures new at that time
was an amiable character from Leeds, rumoured then to be a
fugitive from Butlin's holiday camps or Mecca dance halls,
with an original hair style coloured a bizarre shade of mauve.
His name was Jimmy Savile.

In 1957 I had a telephone call from Barrie Edgar, doyen of the
B.B.C.'s Outside Broadcasts producers in the Midlands. By
then we had worked together on a wide variety of sports and
entertainment programmes, and established a firm rapport.
'I don't suppose,' he said, 'that your tiny mind is capable of
grasping the difference between a samba and a cha-cha-cha?'
I conceded that it certainly was not. 'That's what I thought,'
Mr Edgar went on, 'but would you care to act as compere for
East Midlands in the forthcoming "Come Dancing" series?
All I shall expect you to do is to *look* as if you know what
you're talking about.'

It was always a joy to work with Barrie Edgar. I consulted
my diary and found it somewhat bare of professional
engagements at the appropriate time. But how, I wondered,
might even a one-off assignment of this sort fit in with my
supposedly more rugged role as television's rugby commentator? I took counsel with my personal manager, Edward
Sommerfield, who did not care to be known as a mere agent.
'You do it,' he advised. 'An interesting new challenge, and
who knows where it might lead?' Where indeed? For a start,
to the Nottingham Palais where, if memory serves, East
Midlands survived the first hurdle but bit the dust at the next.

It might be supposed that the compering of a regional
'Come Dancing' team is a piece of cake, yet many good men
and true have come unstuck in the discovery that it is not so
easy as it looks. One of the most successful in that role was
the versatile Alun Williams, who was installed as cheer-
leader for Wales long before I became associated with the
programme. Barrie Edgar thought my two initial performances adequate enough to deserve a further booking for the
following series, when the wheel of fortune spun me
another surprising turn. In my second season East Midlands
became champions, no less, amidst scenes of much local
jubilation. 'On with the dance, let joy be unconfined.'

More crucially, for my part, Barrie's polished regional
production was so highly regarded by mission control in
London that he was offered national charge of the series
next time round. Another of his lively telephone calls
appraised me of the good news. 'I have come to the reluctant conclusion,' he added, 'that having put up with you for
two years in the Midlands I shall now have to endure the
strain on a regular basis. Would you care to preside over the
whole darned shooting match?' This promotion seemed a
reminder yet again of the old adage that it is more often who
rather than what you know that leads to advancement in
life. Yet it was a comfort to have the support and confidence
of an old friend.

To that point 'Come Dancing' had been guided centrally
by a succession of comperes including Peter Dimmock, Paul
Carpenter and then George Elrick from whom I inherited
the chair. Dimmock was front man in the days before he
became head of Outside Broadcasts and presenter of
'Sportsview', a programme in which the driving force of
Paul Fox and Ronnie Noble set new standards on television's
sporting scene. When I had my first walk-on part in Nottingham, Sylvia Peters took charge of the scoreboard in London with the charm expected of someone who had been one
of television's most loved and respected personalities in the
forties and fifties.

(*Left*) Frank Evans, my housemaster and games coach at school – a 'Mr Chips' revered by a host of Old Cranbrookians and remembered with a special affection and respect.

F.W.L. EVANS
(JOE) 1937

(*Below*) The 1938 Cranbrook School rugby XV, unbeaten and led by a captain, slimmer then and with considerably more hair, who believes that all but three of its members remain extant.

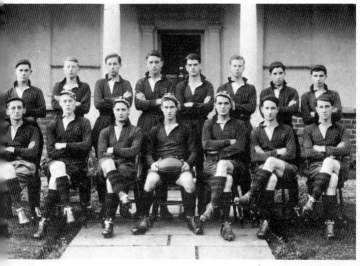

(*Above*) With Harold Gimblett, the great Somerset batsman, at Waterloo Station i
1946 when we said farewell to the first M.C.C. side to tour Australia after the wa

(*Below*) Conversation piece in the fifties with my wife, Pauline, and John
Woodcock, then a young cricket correspondent of *The Times*, whose forthright
and stylish reports for that journal continue to delight his many readers and
admirers.

(*above*) At the Scarborough cricket festival in 1950 – with an illustrious spin-bowling duo, Alfred Valentine (centre) and Sonny Ramadhin, from the West Indies.

(*below*) Another picture from the Scarborough festival, this time of the renowned Yorkshire and England all-rounder, Wilfred Rhodes (centre), in his declining years. (This snapshot is reproduced by courtesy of Geoffrey Copinger whose contributions to the statistics of cricket have been so valuable and respected.)

With my television colleagues, Jim Swanton (left) and Brian Johnston, at the O[...] in 1953 when England won back the Ashes from Australia for the first time [...] the war. The cameraman behind Jim Swanton is Bill Wright who subseque[...] produced the B.B.C.'s popular, long-running series 'Mastermind' until his untimely death.

(*above*) Crawford White, for many years chief cricket reporter for the old *News Chronicle* and then the *Daily Express*, getting some cheerful advice (which he may not have needed) from (left to right) Alec Bedser, then chairman of England's cricket selectors, myself, Trevor Bailey, and Michael Melford, who succeeded Jim Swanton as a highly respected correspondent of the *Daily Telegraph*.

(*below*) Television at Worcester in 1952, when the river Severn flooded the ground and Reg Perks, an England Test cricketer unable to bowl at the touring Indians, brought his fishing rod instead.

(*Above*) With Barrie Edgar (producer) before the televising of a B.B.C. Outside Broadcast series 'Be Your Own Boss' (subsequently re-titled 'Get Ahead') in th' fifties. I worked with Barrie on a wide variety of programmes including, for man' years, 'Come Dancing'. A splendid, unflappable 'pro', and a highly esteemed ol' friend.

(*Below*) Monkey business on a 'Good Companions' TV programme in the fifties

(*above*) A script conference on 'Good Companions' with (left) co-presenter ...nley Dangerfield and producer Humphrey Fisher. 'Good Companions' was ... only programme I worked on which never provoked a rude letter!

(*below*) Linking a 'Come Dancing' programme from the London studio – at a time ...he series when Outside Broadcast cameras covered the competing regions at ...arate venues and the three judges watched it all on a monitor screen.

A stark message displayed on B.B.C. Television during a 'Meeting Point' programme in the sixties.

By the time I was appointed to anchor the show, Sylvia had departed and the efficiency of new scoring procedures rested on my ability to do simple arithmetic. The compere's incompetence in this respect eventually led Barrie Edgar to install the reigning Miss England as mistress of the scoreboard. She might not be able to add up, either, but at least she would introduce a touch of glamour.

The appearance of one Miss England hired for this little chore was not to the liking of an elderly lady viewer in Birmingham. 'Was there any need,' she enquired, 'for that hostess to be nearly naked? It's high time the B.B.C. put a good example in front of their viewers. Yours with her licence paid up.' I thought that for good measure the B.B.C. had paraded two good examples in front of their customers.

There were occasions, to judge from the mail I received, when I might have been presiding over a sexual orgy rather than what one critic described as a soporific screened at an appropriate time of night. 'My friends who go to Community Club,' an anonymous correspondent reported, 'are shocked that those Latin American dancers are turning it into a striptease. Everyone watching can see all they have. Can't it be made a rule to stop this filth? It's embarrassing with a man and teenagers in the house.'

In 1986, 'Come Dancing' was still the longest-running television series in the whole wide world. An essentially familiar, predictable pattern has maintained its popularity in spite of the jive and everything else that has followed since the rock and roll explosion of the fifties. It is colourful and soothing. It introduces for older viewers an element of glamour and romance. It reminds unrepentant oldies such as myself of the days when we got to grips with our partners with practical intent rather than standing off and working ourselves up into an unproductive muck sweat. There is much to be said for the old-fashioned smooch.

Not the least of the programme's virtues – as I was soon to discover – is its competitive flavour. Viewers tend to identify with their own teams, and like to see them win. Some, alas, get extremely upset when their teams lose. In this respect I never had a bleat from Northern Ireland, in spite of the fact that their representatives rarely survived the first round. I had a few complaints from Wales where an outdoor sport I need not identify fires a far greater fervour. Likewise, there were grumbles on occasion from viewers in unsuccessful English regions who, unable to comprehend that the best and most ambitious amateur dancers tended to move to the metropolis, were convinced of judicial prejudice in favour of London teams. But from Scotland I attracted a steady stream of abuse.

I am happy to declare that almost all the Scots I have known personally take modest pleasure from their victories and concede defeat with the best of good grace. I have certainly found this to be the case amongst those close to, say, their rugby scene. There remains a blinkered, nation-alistic and noisy minority north of the border which appar-ently finds it intolerable that a Scottish team should lose to the auld enemy. This applies whether the contest involves rugby, dancing or anything else, including tiddlywinks. So heaven help a wretched Sassenach who had nothing what-ever to do with the final verdict but whose face on 'Come Dancing', week in, week out, was the one immutable fea-ture of the programme.

I soon discovered that one of Scotland's Sunday news-papers was wont to devote its centre spread to complaints about the show – and most of the letters aired grievances about my supposed anti-Scottish prejudices. One of them put it rather neatly. 'We all know Peter West isn't biased,' it read. 'He doesn't really mind who England beats.'

I was held to look delighted when Scotland lost. Perhaps on such occasions I should have worn an air of mourning. I thought I looked equally pleased when announcing Scottish victories, but I never got credit for that. At least I got no snarls when Scotland won.

The fact is that, knowing the pitfalls, craven comperes

and commentators for years have fallen over backwards in their efforts not to be seen as 'anti-Scottish' – to the extent that sometimes they have not been strictly fair to the other side. Dissidents north of the border may never know how much the 'Come Dancing' hierarchy hoped for a Scottish success. It never seemed to occur to blind partisans that an ideal final would involve any two teams from England, Scotland, Wales and Northern Ireland but never two from the same country. From reading the abusive mail it might have been supposed that no region outside London's home counties ever won anything.

Needless to say, the judges on 'Come Dancing', all of them appointed by the official board and all proven experts in their field, also found themselves regularly in the firing line. I suppose this is inevitable if a programme is watched – as it was at its peak of popularity – by nine million judges, most of whom may have felt equally qualified to pronounce an infallible verdict. The official judges, with a reputation to maintain, have never been in a position to deliver an unprofessional decision. I have often known them to be generous to the obviously weaker team: it was a contest, after all, involving amateurs doing their best. But such tolerance, in my experience, never affected the final result.

Such considerations never saved the shining scalp of Scotland's world champion, Bill Irvine, when he gave a judgement against his ain lot. A convivial soul is Bill Irvine – with a fund of stories none of which I dare reproduce here – and an outstanding champion, too. Great Britain has produced the world's best dancers for years and years. Yet the press has remained reluctant to put them in lights.

Some of Irvine's countrymen appear to cultivate anglophobia from a relatively tender age. From Bonnybridge in Stirlingshire came the following charming note: 'I am writing this letter to express my sheer disgust at your pompous attitude and downright cheeky manner of compering a TV show in which Scotland play a part. In Scotland and perhaps elsewhere you are the most disliked of the B.B.C.'s many comperes. I'd like to give you a bit of advice, then. Stop your stupid tom-fooling at once. If you don't, then show your face in certain parts of Scotland and you'll be hung, drawn and quartered. My own bit of advice to you is to stuff yourself with cricket balls. I might add that I'm only fifteen.'

Another letter which got down to instant basics went as follows: 'You conceited, sarcastic, biased English prig. Talk about racial prejudice. Hasn't a look in. Home rule for Scotland! Can't admit or accept defeat. Your smug, sneering façade. Or daren't you enter Scotland? A word of advice, don't ever. Better still, wipe that face off the screen – it distorts it.' By the same post, from Worcestershire: 'We were disgusted that a Scottish judge was chosen when a Scottish team was taking part. The whole show was obviously compered by Peter McWest.' Heigh ho. Not even a friend in Malvern.

Not all the mail from Scotland has been of the style and standard illustrated. I enjoyed the letter from Gourock which suggested that we have Fanny and Johnnie Cradock as judges 'because they're legitimate cooks'. I was less taken by the correspondent from Gorebridge who asked: 'Why don't they have a change of compere now and again instead of you every week? Not that I have anything against you as a person, just your face.'

I had introduced 'Come Dancing' for six series when Barrie Edgar was succeeded as executive maestro by Philip Lewis, who was also based in Birmingham and had taken over the cricket production from Antony Craxton in 1959. So Philip Lewis and I worked closely together, winter and summer, in happy accord until he moved on in 1970 to pastures new. For the past dozen years he has been head of the Entertainment and Events programmes department in London which covers all outside broadcasts, apart from sporting ones, and used to embrace everything from royal occasions at one end of the scale to 'It's a Knock-Out' at the other. Until the programme was lost to the opposition he was able, for a decade and more, to bring his showman's flair to the annual presentation of Miss World.

When Philip Lewis left the 'Come Dancing' programme Barrie Edgar took up the reins once again. Barrie and I did three more series together before, in April 1972, I decided to call it a day. It becomes increasingly difficult for an anchorman to sustain enthusiasm, year in, year out, when working to the same basic script within a format that barely changes. I am not knocking the show on that account: when you have a proven successful formula it does not pay to monkey about with it. There is always a temptation to make a change for change's sake. But the longer I lasted on 'Come Dancing' the more I needed to stick a metaphorical pin into my backside to ensure, if I could, that I appeared to come fresh to the task.

In my early days on the series the show was invariably transmitted 'live'. So, when things went wrong, more often than not it was up to the compere to get things sorted out. We did not often have a serious technical hitch but, when a crisis occurred, I found it a challenge. In fact, I rather enjoyed it when things went wrong. I had not been hired for my dancing expertise, although I suppose it was inevitable that the public thought I knew what I was talking about. But I reckoned I knew something about television.

In due course the show went the way of almost all light entertainment programmes: it was recorded. Henceforth, whenever a hiccup occurred, we stopped and started again. From then on the job somehow seemed less of a challenge and less fun.

As television performers became increasingly specialized it was becoming more and more difficult for me to wear too many hats. For many years I had managed to walk a dangerous tightrope between sports commentary, 'Come Dancing' and a variety of other programmes. I did not think I could hope to sustain the balancing act much longer. I had already been superseded as rugby commentator. Moreover, by the spring of 1972 I was in my first season as rugby football correspondent of *The Times*. Tripping the light fantastic for the telly and writing rugby for the old Thunderer seemed an unlikely mix. So, with all these thoughts in mind, I decided, as it were, to hang up my dancing pumps. My greatest regret lay in parting professional company with an old friend. I felt I was letting him down. Barrie Edgar shared my sorrow but with characteristic buoyancy suggested that I was wise to step down as undefeated cha-cha champion of the south east.

The last 'Come Dancing' final I introduced featured Wales and the North of England in April 1972. Wales (abusive letter writers please note) became the champions. Victor Silvester, the most courtly of men, presented the trophies. A month later I finally bowed out of the terpsichorean scene at the World Professional Championships at the Albert Hall, with Judith Chalmers sharing the commentary. It was nice to finish alongside a true professional with whom I had so often worked. A lovely colleague, Judy: eternally fresh, sincere and cheerful.

After it was all over, someone from B.B.C. 2's 'Late Night Line-up' programme telephoned to ask whether I would care to be interviewed by Joan Bakewell while dancing with her in front of the cameras. I said that no one could admire Ms Bakewell more than I but had no hesitation in declining the invitation with thanks.

Some of my coarse rugby friends have asked me how it was I managed to survive the dancing scene so long. I always turned the question by wondering whether the dancing fraternity might not have been justified in resenting the intrusion of a muddied oaf into their particular world. If it did, it scarcely ever showed. I was grateful for the welcome and the help I had from such delightful people as Frank and Peggy Spencer, whose formation teams contributed so much to what was always the most popular part of the show. I should add, too, that it was a regular pleasure to work with Joe Loss, for whom no rehearsal, no attention to detail and preparation, was ever too much. A great old 'pro'

– and Ray McVay was an outstanding younger one.

Mecca's Eric Morley, who organized and staged 'Come Dancing', combined with the B.B.C. to give me a generous farewell party as well as a handsome pair of drinking cups which have been regularly put to excellent use. I could look back on fourteen years in the hot seat, and two more on the regional fringes. In 1964, dinner-jacketed and looking rather too sleek, I had even appeared on the cover of *Radio Times*. I would rather have had a cricket bat or rugby ball in my hand, but beggars can't be choosers.

In 1962, to my genuine amazement, I had been called up at the end of the televised Carl Alan Awards to receive, for that year, the trophy for 'outstanding services to ballroom dancing'. I hope I made it publicly clear that the award had been given to a front man representing Barrie Edgar and all the others involved in the television effort. I was delighted that in later years Barrie and Phil Lewis both received the special Carl Alan Award. Barrie's was in celebration of his twenty-fifth year in association with the 'Come Dancing' programme.

If Eric Morley made a long and crucial contribution, back stage, to the 'Come Dancing' series he played a bigger, more publicized part in the annual televised extravaganza, Miss World. 'I will announce the last three in reverse order,' he says. It became his catch phrase.

Brought up in a hard school – he had been an Army band boy – Eric Morley, in the days when I first knew him, waged intermittent war with a succession of B.B.C. producers, mustered his Miss World contestants with an iron hand and no obvious velvet glove and sometimes drove them to tears at rehearsal. But an often harsh, abrasive exterior masked a kindly nature: a rough diamond who always came up with the goods. I think we treated each other with a sort of wary respect. For my part that respect soon turned to an affectionate regard.

I did not often agree with the judges' verdict on the Miss World programmes, but it would be a complicated planet if we all had the same taste. However, in my book the judiciary certainly got it right when they elected Miss Jamaica in the sixties – and thereby hangs a little tale.

Miss Jamaica did not conform to conventional notions of a beauty queen. She was stunning, petite, and wore at the final rehearsal a very sexy leather swimsuit, low cut with a zipper down to its nether regions. The entire B.B.C. television crew had put its money on this enchanting sorceress from the Caribbean when I confided to her that in *that* outfit she could not possibly lose. 'Oh,' she said. 'I was going to wear something else for the show.' 'I'm telling you,' I replied, 'you'll be daft if you do.' She took my advice, won by the proverbial street and was thoughtful enough to send me a thank you postcard after her triumphant return to Kingston.

Talking to Miss Jamaica 'live' on television made for one of the rare interviews I enjoyed on the Miss World programmes. That is more than I can say about a chat I had with one of her victorious predecessors, who had halitosis. I remember Anthony Newley looking in at the Lyceum rehearsals before Miss Jamaica was crowned. Someone suggested he was giving one of his old hit songs a new title: *Stop Miss World, I want to get on*.

Chapter Four

For a record programme entitled 'Morning Call', which went out on the B.B.C.'s old Light Programme, I devised a gimmick suggesting the presence in the studio of the family's Airedale (who rejoiced in the not very original name of Lassie). Doggie noises, artificially produced, were effective enough to persuade a number of listeners that Lassie was my constant companion on the show. But not, I suspect, the one who wrote, 'Why don't you let that dog choose the records – while *you* take a long walk?'

On another programme, 'Motoring and the Motorist', I was unwise enough, when the talk was about pedestrian crossings, to relate a story of which I am rather fond. This concerned a blind man, accompanied by his guide dog, who was waiting for a break in the traffic. The dog took occasion to raise one leg and piddle down his owner's trousers, whereupon the blind man was seen by a bystander to fiddle in his macintosh pocket before giving the dog a biscuit. This was more than the bystander could take in silence. 'I'm amazed,' he said. 'That dog of yours has just wetted your trousers and yet you give him a biscuit.' 'Why don't you mind your own business?' the blind man retorted. 'I'm finding out which end is which before I kick it up the backside.'

This story brought the programme to a happy conclusion for the studio audience. It also brought several letters to my producer protesting about the chairman's insensitivity. 'Mr

West must surely know,' said one, 'that a blind man would never kick his guide dog under any circumstances.' It all went to show how careful one has to be.

After the untimely death of Franklin Engelmann I was asked by the B.B.C. if I was interested to have my name considered as his successor on 'Down Your Way'. It was a programme I would have loved to do, but other commitments obliged me to decline this invitation. The assignment went to my old chum, Brian Johnston, and the B.B.C. could not have made a better choice. Brian must have turned his versatile hand to a greater variety of radio broadcasts than any other man – as his highly successful forays into authorship have confirmed. He has presided over 'Down Your Way' with the unfailing good cheer, spontaneity and genuine humility which have been the hallmark of his work.

To radio, in which Brian Johnston long since became an immensely popular 'institution' – and always his own man – I have made relatively spasmodic contributions. As I look back, I can say that none of them shaped my future career more productively than those I made for the old 'Sports Report' programme introduced by Eamonn Andrews and produced by Angus Mackay.

The partnership of Eamonn in front of the microphone with Mackay masterminding the operation set new standards in sports reporting on radio. I was lucky in my formative years to be taken on by Mackay as one of his team and to learn the skill of delivering a report to the exact length demanded. Armed with a scripted piece lasting a required minute and a half, I learnt to be flexible when Angus Mackay ordained a cut of thirty seconds as I arrived in the studio and another fifteen more just as I was about to deliver it. He could be a difficult man to work for, and eventually, after a number of years, I joined a long list of those who had been dropped from his programme. I felt pretty sick about it at the time. I thought I had served him loyally and efficiently. But in retrospect I have to say that he was an immense professional who taught me some essential broadcasting disciplines.

I have lost count of the number and variety of televised Outside Broadcasts – apart from sport – I did in the fifties and sixties. But I recall two series with special pleasure. One of them was 'Be Your Own Boss', subsequently retitled 'Get Ahead', and the other was 'Good Companions'.

'Be Your Own Boss', a competition for entrepreneurs enthusiastic but lacking the means to set themselves up in a new business venture, was the brainchild of the old *News Chronicle*. Barrie Edgar, with whom I worked not just on 'Come Dancing' but on every sort of Outside Broadcast from sport to circuses, was the producer when it was first televised. When it was retitled it was also planned to introduce a new chairman, Kenneth Horne, a tycoon of commerce in his own right. But he suffered an untimely stroke, and I was reprieved. So was Viscountess Lewisham, a member of the judging panel who survived shrieks of protest from the Labour party on the grounds that she was Tory candidate for West Lewisham in the London County Council elections. I do not know whether the television exposure was any help to her candidature, but she seemed never without an instant if not very profound opinion on any topic for discussion.

In later series she was succeeded by Mrs John Profumo (the former actress, Valerie Hobson) who charmingly contributed some thoughtful points amongst the heavyweight business expertise of men such as Sir Miles Thomas and Sir Frederic Hooper, bosses respectively of BOAC and Schweppes. I remember some trenchant contributions from William Hardcastle in the days before this hard-bitten Fleet Street editor became a regular broadcaster. Another of the judges was J. G. W. (Jack) Davies, a financial expert forever remembered in cricket circles as the Cambridge undergraduate who bowled the great Don Bradman for nought.

For some years 'Get Ahead' was a regular annual series, which confirmed its success and popularity. So was 'Good Companions', a programme about household pets which was screened in the early evening and attracted a loyal audience. 'Good Companions', which I introduced in alliance with Stanley Dangerfield, a pillar of the Kennel Club, put its main emphasis on dogs, who could be relied on to play a lively if unpredictable part.

The noble head of a Great Dane may not be everyone's idea of the perfect television close-up but I can think of a great many worse. As a dog lover I felt in my element, and I had a trusted colleague to supply the expertise. We covered the Cruft's show together a number of times but that was a more formal occasion involving the best of breeds. For my money the organized chaos of pedigree and mongrel on 'Good Companions' was always more entertaining. And the frequent presence of children on the programme made it more appealing.

To have Humphrey Fisher as a relaxed yet very professional producer was another plus. I worked under Humphrey for several years at Wimbledon, on the 'Get Ahead' series, and on heaven knows what else. He is one of the six sons of Lord Fisher, former Archbishop of Canterbury, all of whom achieved distinction in their varied lives. An agnostic if not a positive atheist, Humphrey was none the less done proud by his old man who married him off in Lambeth Palace. Mr and Mrs West, arriving late for the ceremony, blotted their copybooks by sneaking up the aisle just as the Archbishop was making his entrance.

Humphrey's bride was Diana, a lovely, effervescent lady who was not known by her friends as 'Dizzy Di' for nothing. She subsequently made a considerable name for herself in Australian television and radio, and dispensed generous hospitality to all their old friends who happened to land up in Sydney. Humphrey was one of the senior Outside Broadcast producers when the B.B.C. sent him in 1964 to represent the Corporation in Australia. Three years later he returned to the domestic fold as Head of Science and Features for B.B.C. Television, but I suspect he grew tired of the politics which seems to bedevil all big organizations. He had certainly liked Australia, its people and its climate. So he went back there on a permanent basis, and joined the Australian Broadcasting Commission in 1969. He comes home rarely these days, but Diana makes her annual pilgrimage to Wimbledon, Ascot and other up-market occasions, regaling readers of her weekly column in a Sydney Sunday newspaper with details of how the other half lives it up.

'Good Companions' was still a popular early evening show when Donald Baverstock, the head of B.B.C. 1, decreed that enough was enough. I was told he did not think it a 'hard enough' programme, so he took it off the air. Ye gods, was there no room under a new regime for something a bit soft and sentimental? Some years later the B.B.C. tried another programme called 'Dog Watch', and asked me to introduce it. It was too clinical, too contrived and by the time almost every item had been recorded about half a dozen times to satisfy a producer reluctant to accept a fresh and early 'take', it was a moot point whether the dogs or the human beings were more jaded. This programme did, however, produce a golden moment at Spiller's Nutritional Centre where a test was conducted to find out which of three different dog-meats was preferred. A toffee-nosed poodle sniffed the three plates, lifted a leg and put the seal of his disapproval on one of them.

I had no reservations about a programme devised and produced by Brian Robins. In the early sixties, 'What's New?' did for younger viewers what 'Tomorrow's World' was later to achieve for a wider audience. It was a joy to work on it along with Polly Elwes and Brian Johnston – and a young man who had been making a mark in Bristol and was now spreading his wings on a networked programme for the first time. None of us doubted that he would be heard of again. His name was David Dimbleby.

In the late fifties, when I was flitting from one programme to another, the *Sunday Express* under a headline 'Black out these TV bores' devoted several trenchant columns to the subject of Bob McKenzie, Peter Haigh, Jeanne Heal and yours truly, who was rated at number four in the hit list.

'Is Mr Peter West reading this?' enquired Peter Buchan. 'Did he imagine I would leave him out of the list of the Four Biggest Bores? West has become one of the inescapable faces of television. He started as a cricket commentator in which his knowledge was more important than his manner. From there he went to compering amateur shows – a job which needs a smooth, accomplished performer able to set new-comers to TV at their ease. West looked more embarrassed than the contestants. Since then he has described dogs, met monkeys and lions, taken the chair at parlour games, commented on swimming spectacles, and even told the story of Alcock and Brown's transatlantic flight.

'Through it West has worn an invariable three-inch grin, a half-lowered head and, most irritating of all, a pipe which flits from pocket to hand to mouth and back to his pocket. West now brings his pipe to "Box Office", I.T.V.'s rival to "Picture Parade". And when that and his smile fail to bore, West fumbles through explanations of film plots in a man-ner reminiscent of a schoolgirl telling her bestest friend about the flick she saw the night before.

'What is to be done about the TV bores? For the sake of television as a medium of entertainment I suggest that the B.B.C. and I.T.V. get together and send them into exile, taking their wisdom, pomposity, sympathy and smiles with them. Not for too long of course. Say 100 years.'

I can't say this made for the happiest breakfast reading in the West household. Within hours, however, there arrived a telephoned cable from my manager, Edward Sommerfield, who was sunning himself in the South of France. 'Congratu-lations,' it went, 'I couldn't have bought the space.'

In the fifteen years of my association with Teddy Sommerfield I only once remember him telling me to turn a job down when it involved some visual exposure. I cannot forget that he, as well as Eamonn Andrews, had been largely instrumental in my being cast, for one night only, on 'What's My Line?' – an event which changed the course of my television career. I was, so he assured me then, the favoured colt in his stable. In many ways he did me proud. But eventually, after a rift with Eamonn, he set up a new management company without so much as a letter or a telephone call to tell me what he had done.

There is a timeless adage that in show-biz, so long as your name is spelt right, it is better to be insulted than ignored. We have all heard the stories of an American entertainer, his latest show panned by all the critics, who announced that he would cry all the way to the bank – or of another who read the cuttings and said simply, 'It's sad that only the public like me.'

I consoled myself with reading another criticism which held that I was rather solemn, with a tendency to glower at the cameras as though I wished them some personal harm. But yet another was back on the opposite tack: 'He wears a patent leather parting and a three-inch grin.' I had hair in those days.

I did not enjoy any of these strictures but had to concede that the critics were entitled to their opinions. Nor did I like what Ramsden Greig wrote about me in London's *Evening Standard* a few years later. Mr Greig announced on the telephone that he wanted to write a feature about me. I wish, with the benefit of hindsight, that I had not been so foolish as to invite him to dinner. He appeared to enjoy the meal, and it was gratifying to see him indulge a distinctly healthy thirst.

Observe how a columnist, clawing through the library files, can feed off the bile of his colleagues. When his feature appeared in print it was at once apparent that he had done his homework. In one respect he felt able to paint the lily. 'Peter West is the B.B.C. TV and radio commentator with the patent leather parting and the *four*-inch smile (my italics). He is not to be confused with the B.B.C.'s other Peter (Haigh), who is the one with the patent leather smile and the four-inch parting.' All good readable stuff.

'Mr West,' the piece went on, 'does the commentaries on

rugby, tennis, hockey, lacrosse, rowing, etc, etc. On the screens and on the air he has also talked about dogs, interviewed monkeys, chaired panel games and described the net and sequins brigade who inhabit the programme "Come Dancing". He is, in short, The Great Inescapable. He was once described by a columnist, who is no fan, as the Fourth Biggest Bore on TV.'

Now for the first manufactured 'quote'. '"I was terribly put out," West says. "I don't like coming fourth in anything." He heads you across the dining room of his home in Petts Wood to a cupboard full of silver cups. "There are twenty of them," he says. "There are twenty-two of them," says his wife, who has to polish them. West says: "Won most of them at my public school, Cranbrook, you know: I captained the school at cricket, rugger, hockey, fives and athletics. Now I am one of the governors and it's all I can do to take the dog out for a brisk walk."'

This was good imaginative going, all of it designed to create an impression the writer intended to convey. I had not drawn his attention to the cups. I supplied no details of my athletic career at school until I was asked. But on with the fabricated 'quotes'.

'He takes you into the lounge to fill the inevitable pipe and says: "I do my first Boat Race commentary for the B.B.C. this year. I suppose you could call that something of an accolade. I'll please some people. But I fully expect to get the usual batch of letters telling me to get that damn smug smile off my face."

'It is difficult to remove a smug smile when you are earning around £14,000 a year, have two cars in the garage, you own private cricket pitch and a swimming pool on order for your back garden.' By now, Mr Greig was excelling himself in flights of fancy. I had declined to tell him what my income was, the 'private cricket pitch' was a half-net for my two lads at one end of a lawn which measured some twenty yards by twelve. There was little room for a swimming pool, and I certainly did not have one on order.

I have alluded in some detail to this example of clever but unprincipled journalism not just because it has stuck in my craw, but because it might serve as a useful warning to other potential victims. Looking back through my press cuttings I come to a reluctant conclusion that I have had my share of stick, almost all of it fair comment and I dare say much of it justified. I have had, thank the good Lord, plenty of kindly comments too.

No critic in my early days in television gave me a more consistent thumbs down for extra-curricular (non-sporting) activities than Peter Black of the *Daily Mail*. But I retained a considerable respect for his judgement, his knowledge of the medium and his always constructive approach. Maurice Wiggin of the *Sunday Times* was another for whom I had the highest regard, but he was consistently kind to me and no doubt I am prejudiced in his favour as a result. Herbert Kretzmer, the present *Daily Mail* television critic, is another I rate very highly. To the best of my knowledge he has never written anything about me, so in his case I should have no bias, conscious or otherwise.

No critic has written more entertainingly than Clive James, whose weekly television piece in the *Observer* used to make for a brilliant, essential read. Nowadays, of course, he paints a wider canvas. But in his time as a TV critic I never thought he was much interested in constructive comment, certainly not about sporting programmes. It so happens that Clive James is an Australian not apparently interested in cricket. He aimed his arrows elsewhere, as David Vine may testify. David Vine is a splendidly efficient and trustworthy front man. Nothing – outwardly at least – will ruffle his composure in the nastiest crisis. Yet if Mr James had an inkling of the pressures to which Vine is constantly subject, it never showed in print.

Television finds itself unable to take up the cudgels on behalf of its sometimes maligned performers, and sport suffers more than most departments in this way. Sometimes it also gets a raw deal from journalists reporting sport day in day out who, though they may not admit it, are envious of the status and impact of television and disgruntled by the privileges they see are attached to it. He who pays the piper is entitled now and then to call the tune.

If I make these observations while wearing two distinctively different hats, I had only one on my balding head when helping to lighten a Sabbath for readers of the *News of the World*. In the late summer of 1964 we took a family holiday at the Villamil Hotel in Paguera on the southern coast of Majorca. Peter Dimmock, then head of B.B.C. Outside Broadcasts, and his wife, Polly Elwes, were also there along with several of their friends.

The hour of midnight loomed towards the end of a distinctly convivial party by the swimming pool when the B.B.C.'s HOB suggested it would be fun to indulge in a midnight swim in the all-together. This seemed a very good idea indeed, not least because one member of our party was a gorgeous creature (divorced from her husband) whom I shall not name for fear of hearing from her solicitor. So down to the beach we go and in no time at all we are all cavorting about in the water as mother nature intended. This sort of activity would be regarded as par for the course in an age when even German hausfraus parade their topless armaments on the beach, but in those days it was not well regarded by the local constabulary. And, as ill-luck would have it, a Spanish beach patrol came by.

What was more unfortunate, the corporal in charge of it had obviously just won promotion and was anxious to prove something. There ensued a mildly hilarious passage while the gendarmerie confiscated our clothes on the beach. We stayed paddling in deepish water while friends who had observed the crisis develop rushed off to fetch towels so that we might arise from the sea with some pretence of dignity. The Villamil's head waiter, Jackie, who was known to exert considerable influence, was also summoned to take charge of the peace talks.

At these he did such a persuasive job that we were

allowed to retrieve our clothes and return to our respective rooms. What official action might be taken in the morning we were left to contemplate. For the moment, back to the hotel, to enjoy the Fundador and Calisay.

At that stage I was unaware of the fact that Peter Dimmock, at the first sign of danger, and with some enterprise, had made a bunk for it out of the water. He sped off for reinforcements, and rumour had it that he was last seen starkers in the headlights of a car passing the hotel's front door.

It was subsequently revealed that a member of the party had filched the corporal's greatcoat as a trophy of war. The consequences were unfortunate. Understandably put out, the corporal returned next morning to insist that all our passports should be impounded. It was no joke now. But after lengthy negotiations with the police our magnificent head waiter arranged an uneasy armistice and all passports, even that of our chief criminal, were allowed to stay with us.

I remember thinking at the time that the story of Dimmock and West, two men in the public eye back home, would make an interesting paragraph or two if the news got out. Some six weeks later I had virtually forgotten the incident when, having finished my commentary on a rugby match in Cardiff, I was told there was a telephone call for me in the TV production 'scanner'. 'Is that Peter West?' a voice enquired. I said it was. 'I am speaking to you from the *News of the World*. I understand you were involved in a nude bathing party at the Villamil Hotel in Majorca on the night of September 17. Can you confirm this?' There are moments in life when we all need to think pretty damn quick. The reporter had the essential facts. If I denied my presence and was later proved a liar, much good would that do me. My wife had been with me, so it all seemed quite respectable. 'Yes,' I replied. 'I was.'

I supplied more details when pressed but, although conceding that the beach party had consisted of English guests at the hotel, declined to name anyone else. 'But we are told

83

that Peter Dimmock was one of them,' the reporter went on. 'I am not naming names,' I said. Stiff upper lip and all that.

On my drive back to London's south east suburbs I reflected that the story might rate a few inches on one of the middle pages. My wife was spending the evening with friends. The telephone rang as I opened the front door of our home in Bickley. 'This is the picture desk of the *News of the World*,' another voice said. 'We would like to send a photographer to get a shot of you and your wife.' I temporized; things seemed to be getting out of hand. 'Ring me back in ten minutes,' I said.

I took immediate counsel with Edward Sommerfield, who knew more about these affairs than I did. 'No,' he enjoined. 'I think things have gone far enough. Don't agree to a photo.' But I might as well have been hung for a sheep as a lamb. A big story from the United States was the lead on page one of the morrow's *News of the World*. Number two, prominently featured, had the headlines: 'Peter West in nude swim party.' The reporter, Roger Hall, wrote a fair and accurate account of our conversation on the telephone. It included another paragraph which went as follows: 'In Majorca the story was that Peter Dimmock, head of BBC Outside Broadcasts, and his wife, Polly Elwes, were also in the party, but Mr Dimmock said last night: "It sounds to me like a rumour magnified out of all proportion. I know of no such party."'

Several daily newspapers followed up a possible lead the next day, but with a nerveless and enviable sangfroid Peter Dimmock stuck to his account and that was that. I wished I had taken the same bold line. Yet if I had scotched the tale at birth, it would not have made much of a story for me now.

In the early fifties I was offered the opportunity of applying for a staff appointment as the Outside Broadcasts radio producer, with opportunities for commentary, in what was then the B.B.C.'s north region. I have sometimes wondered how things would have turned out if I had not declined the offer, and had been accepted for the job. It went to Robert Hudson, who subsequently became the very efficient head of radio's Outside Broadcasts in London. In our early days we shared cricket broadcasts. He is still, in his retirement, adorning the air waves with his cultured commentaries on State occasions.

At the time when I turned that offer down O.B. producers and commentators on the B.B.C.'s staff were nothing like so well paid – in comparison with outside contributors – as they are these days. I was then earning a considerably better crust as a free-lance, albeit with no guarantee as to future employment and no provision for a pension in my dotage apart from any personal arrangements I might sensibly make out of an unpredictable income.

A successful career as a free-lance in radio and TV – or in journalism come to that – calls, I think, for a combination of professional expertise, self-confidence, determination and luck. I started with good times in television which got even better before I suffered a longish period in which I wondered how I might manage to pay the mortgage and sustain family standards while our three children were being educated.

Edward Sommerfield's advice as my manager for fifteen years was always that I should resist the temptation to ask the B.B.C. for an exclusive contract guaranteeing a specified minimum annual income. 'Be independent, my boy,' he affirmed, 'and make a lot more.' This advice turned out for a long while to be sound enough. 'Gather ye rosebuds while ye may.' But who knows when the good times, for whatever reason, may suddenly end?

There is always the temptation for a free-lance never to turn down the offer of work. There have been things which in retrospect I would rather not have done, but for a long time I saw no prospect of making a decent living in sport alone. In later years, I was happy to accept an exclusive contract with the B.B.C. for cricket on the box and rugby on the air.

By then, in what I thought was a prudent safeguard for the future, this free-lance had dipped his toe into different waters. An old friend, John Newman, asked me to join him in a newly-formed firm of insurance brokers, but because of other commitments I failed to pull my weight. Our partnership ended in amity. Subsequently, in the late sixties, I was introduced to a young man, Patrick Nally, and invited to form with him the public relations arm of a small advertising agency.

The ambitious Patrick, then still in his early twenties and working for one of the big agencies, was looking for pastures new. He was a salesman to his finger tips, a workaholic steeped in PR and advertising, and teeming with ideas. His far less creative partner was familiar with the sporting scene at a time when sports sponsorship had begun to spread its wings, and his versatile background in the media was a useful plus. It seemed a promising alliance. We guided Benson and Hedges, who were looking to make an important mark in sponsorship, to Lord's and the launching of cricket's new league competition in 1972, and we persuaded Green Shield to take on a tennis sponsorship at grass roots level which I am certain, but for their trading traumas, would be continuing to this day.

The success of the West Nally Group, long since established in Berkeley Square House, with offices world-wide, was built on servicing sports sponsorships in this country and then expanded by Patrick Nally's tireless efforts overseas. While I contented myself with overseeing the domestic front, Patrick, exceeding even the flying hours of Dr Kissinger as he travelled the globe, enlisted the support of key multi-national companies in the marketing of a host of important international events. At football's World Cup tournaments in Argentina (1978) and in Spain (1982) his marketing concept, original then, was to sell promotional rights to a limited number of companies, all of them exclusive within their own field.

West Nally now act officially, or have acted, for many

international or UK based sports bodies. They do not get their wires crossed by representing individual sportsmen or women, and I dare say this was one of the reasons why they acquired, on behalf of the International Rugby Board, the marketing rights for the game's first World Cup, in New Zealand and Australia in 1987. Their efforts in marketing Twickenham for the Rugby Football Union, at a time of economic down-turn in Britain, had been more successful than some critics were prepared to concede.

Before resigning from West Nally at Christmas 1983, and settling for a quieter life, I had derived a lot of satisfaction from presiding over a low-key but subtly effective campaign to get Cornhill's Test cricket sponsorship on the road. When Karen Earl, a fellow director, left at the same time to set up shop on her own, she took, with Patrick Nally's blessing, the Benson and Hedges and Cornhill accounts with her and now oversees their affairs with charm and efficiency.

I want in particular to place on record my special appreciation of the loyalty of Leonard Owen, Special Events Director of Benson and Hedges, who unswervingly supported us throughout the good and the testing times. He has never wavered in his insistence that everything Benson and Hedges put their stamp on in sport should be touched by genuine quality. If their cricket sponsorship remains the flagship, the Benson and Hedges tennis and snooker tournaments, now totally organized by Karen Earl Limited, under Leonard Owen's supervision, stand as examples of sporting events admirably staged and highly esteemed by players and public.

Chapter Five

'WE ALWAYS KNOW IT'S raining when we see your ugly mug on the box.' Thus spoke one of my blunt acquaintances with, I had to concede, a fair measure of truth. If rain or bad light stopped play, more often than not this anchorman was in business.

Nick Hunter, the B.B.C.'s senior cricket producer, and his aides come to every televised game prudently armed with relevant tapes of other matches and wet weather contingency plans, which need to be flexible. There is no point in opting for half an hour of a recording if the break seems likely to be a brief one. At such times I have been grateful to my colleagues, who help me bridge the gap.

There is no shortage of interesting topics for discussion; the play so far (with visual illustrations), the state of the game, what is likely to unfold. One of our commentators will be chatting about this and that, and I will be seeking to keep things going while receiving information, guidance and instruction from my producer through a 'deaf aid'. Before we go on the air with an interview there is verbal contact with the producer through what we call a 'lazy mike'. But once he has cued his presenter to action, communication – producer to presenter – is one way only.

There are times when a presenter's life becomes distinctly fraught. On the one hand he is seeking to listen attentively to what, for instance, Tom Graveney is saying, before posing a follow-up question of reasonable intelligence. On the other he might be receiving in his lug hole a change of plan the details of which must be rapidly assimilated. He hopes to convey a bland impression of hanging on Thomas's every word yet in fact is concentrating like mad on what his producer is telling him. In such situations anchormen have something in common with Jekyll and Hyde.

Through his 'deaf aid' there will always come, from the producer's assistant, a count-down to the end of every transmission. 'Five minutes, four minutes,' and so on, until the last seconds when it becomes, 'Ten, nine, eight,' until death us do part. No professional worth his salt knowingly or willingly signs off except on the dot. In this respect I had a problem at the Nat West final in 1983.

During interviews at the end of the match it became clear that I was hearing nothing from the producer, Bill Taylor – and no count-down either. Trusting the good Lord to provide, I ploughed on regardless and, having talked with the two captains, Ian Botham and Chris Tavare, thought it right to introduce the man of the match, Vic Marks. This decision coincided with a vigorous cut-your-throat signal from one of our stage managers which implied that we had run out of time and had better get off the air pretty damned quick. I congratulated Victor on his performance and said farewell from Lord's in the same breath. The man of the match was entitled to look startled. He never got a word in.

This hiccup duly appeared in that winter's 'Sports Review of the Year' on the sure premise that viewers enjoy nothing more than seeing us get our knickers in a twist. Something comparable occurred a year or two earlier at The Oval when my conversation with the umpires, Bill Alley and Tom Spencer, was drowned by a public address announcement belted out through a loudspeaker a few feet above our heads.

Coping with extraneous noise can be testing enough even when communications – producer to presenter – are working well (as they almost always do). At the climax of a one-day final, and sometimes of a Test series, the winning team's supporters make such a din it is difficult to hear yourself think, let alone pick up what the captains are saying or the advice coming into an ear from your producer.

In this respect I have had some challenging times at Headingley where the balcony is very close to the crowd gathered for the presentations. But it has been a big plus for us there that we have sometimes achieved an immediate interview with the hero of the hour. When Geoffrey Boycott came off the field after completing his hundredth hundred in the Australian Test of 1977 it made ideal television to have him talking, in front of his own kingdom, before he had taken off his pads. Not long before that he had talked to me in front of the cameras after making another Test century – and running out Derek Randall when that ebullient character had embarked on a first Test innings on his own ground. Not the best thing for our Geoffrey to have done at Trent Bridge. But he then surprised a few people by making handsome confession of his guilt.

When a minimum number of overs has to be bowled in a day's Test play it tends to make TV and radio planning difficult if not impossible. It also frustrates journalists conscious of deadlines and edition times. But if play goes the distance to an advertised closing time, television – in theory at least – usually has five minutes for a review of the day's proceedings. In practice, of course, the last over – perhaps from a fast bowler – may start just before the stumps are due to be pulled out.

This calls for some flexibility from all concerned, notably Nick Hunter, whose editorial judgements must constantly alter as the clock ticks on. For the benefit of those coming home from work he will probably have shown them, between the last overs of the day, how the earlier wickets fell. Come the last judgement, it is sometimes a case of one or two more illustrations, a rapid twosome in vision and the anchorman's firm tap on someone's toes as indication that time is up.

I wish I had kept a tally of all the players I have talked to during televised cricket. There was a day in 1980 at the Cornhill Centenary Test so bedevilled by the weather that interviews, live or recorded, went on for three or four hours. Old adversaries – Compton and Miller, Benaud and May, Lock and Harvey, Laker and Davidson, Hutton and Hassett – locked horns again in genial and absorbing reminiscence. None were more venerable than P. G. H. Fender, the oldest surviving England Test cricketer, then eighty-eight, and 'Stork' Hendry, the senior Australian at the celebration, a very lively eighty-five. I spoke to them in the garden behind the Warner stand, and for a minute or two found it difficult to spark off a nostalgic momentum.

Stork Hendry suddenly remarked to Percy George that when he had batted against his leg breaks in 1921 the bowler had used a deep fine leg. 'No, no, no', Percy George affirmed. 'I had him square.' From that moment on they were immersed in old memories, fighting old battles, oblivious of the cameras or a third party.

Another famous Surrey and England player, Andy Sandham, then eighty-nine, was not strong enough to attend the Centenary at Lord's. Shortly before that contest, however, Nick Hunter contrived to get him in front of a camera at the Oval. He also persuaded Ben Travers, the playwright, to join the conversation.

Mr Travers, a cricket fanatic then well into his nineties, discoursed on 'W.G.' and the Golden Age. At length, the conversation having moved on to Bradman and other illustrious captains, I thought it time to elicit opinions about another outstanding leader who was also a great all-rounder. 'What,' I asked Andy Sandham, 'about Richie Benaud?' Andy paused for reflection. 'Benaud?' he said. 'I don't think I know anything about 'im.' This reply caused great joy in our commentary box.

Almost all cricketers, of whatever generation, talk with interest and enthusiasm about their game. Yet there was an occasion at Headingley in 1981 when the top brass in

England's side seemed reluctant to speak with the media about a famous victory over Australia. This was at a time when Mike Brearley, Bob Willis and Ian Botham (there may have been others) were conducting a private war with a section of the popular Press. The details of this conflict seem even less important now, and I will only observe that legions of fine players have managed to endure such problems in the past without threatening to send some members of the media to Coventry – a fate which I dare say some of them have deserved.

It was inevitable, I suppose, that the quarrel Brearley and company were having with the Press rubbed off to some extent on television and radio journalists. However, interviews with all sections of the media after a Test match is finished are seen as an obligatory part of the captain's role. Brearley did his stuff in front of a camera on the Headingley balcony, as eventually did Botham, whose magnificent 149 not out in England's second innings had turned the match on its head when their cause seemed hopeless. 'It just shows,' Ian said, with a glint in his eye, 'that the media should never have written us off.' 'In that case,' I replied, hoping to make the score 15-all, 'why did the England team check out of their hotel this morning?'

In the previous Test at Lord's Botham had bagged a pair of noughts and, bowing to some remorseless pressures, had surrendered the England captaincy. So how much easier had it been for him to play that astonishing innings at Headingley? Did he feel a great weight had been lifted off his shoulders? He gave me a long and measured look. 'That's the Catch 22 question,' he replied, without further elaboration. I do not think he has ever wavered from a belief that he ought to be England's captain still.

Amongst the melee on the balcony that giddy day in Leeds there was no sign of Bob Willis, whose superb bowling (8 for 43) had clinched the result at the climax of the match. It was clear that we ought not to sign off on television without a few words from another English hero. I approached the captain, seeking permission for another interview. 'Bob's in the bath,' Mike Brearley said. 'You can ask him yourself.'

At this point I must explain that my relationship with Robert George Dylan Willis had been somewhat strained since the Nottingham Test of the previous summer. Against the West Indies at Trent Bridge he had bowled outstandingly well yet endured a day when the batsmen played and missed, and almost everything had gone wrong for him. I waited for him, by the pavilion gate, at close of play – and soon discovered I was pushing my luck. Storming past me with a glazed, unyielding glare, he told me where I could put the suggested interview.

Our next meeting was in the indoor school at Lord's where Cornhill dispense hospitality at the end of a Test match. I played the first insensitive stroke. 'I know you'd had a hard day at Nottingham,' I observed, 'but we all have a job to do and I don't see why you had to be so bloody rude and uncooperative.' 'Oh,' said Robert, 'in that case I'm off.' Whereupon he turned on his heels and departed in high dudgeon.

This then was the background when at Headingley in 1981 I knocked on the door of the England dressing room and was bidden to enter. Stretched out in a bath absurdly small for his elongated figure lay the fast bowler, contemplating his navel. 'Bob,' I said. 'Well bowled. Tremendous. Will you come and talk to me on the tube?' He gave me another of those searching looks. 'What,' he replied, 'about Lord's last year?' This struck me as being an unproductive start to our conversation. 'Surely we can forget that,' I went on. 'It's been a marvellous day for English cricket.' Bob thought about it again. 'All right,' he said. 'I'll be with you in five minutes.'

Duly appearing in front of a camera, he knocked the wind out of my sails and, to judge from the mail I subsequently received, astounded many viewers by launching himself into a condemnation of the media. We were still 'live' on the

94

air; it struck me at once that talk of this kind was wildly inappropriate to the occasion. I interrupted his flow. 'Bob,' I said, 'you've just won a Test match in the most remarkable circumstances. Can't we stick to a happier topic?' This, I am glad to recall, diverted him to a much more acceptable theme.

Much good did it do me in one respect. In a later feature in *The Times* it was written that Willis, 'having punctuated the ultimate triumph by delivering a coruscating general denunciation to a squirming Peter West in front of the B.B.C.'s cameras on the Headingley balcony, withdrew from journalists altogether.'

I permit myself the rare luxury of quoting from two kindly letters. One came from my old radio boss, Lobby (Seymour de Lotbiniere). 'I find myself rejoicing that C. B. (Fry) so successfully thrust you towards the B.B.C. some thirty and more years ago – and today, after seeing you eventually forcing a smile out of Bob Willis, my satisfaction reached its zenith.' The other was from Humphrey Burton, a doyen of television arts programmes, whom I have never met. 'I thought you were magnificent with Bob Willis this afternoon, turning a very nasty argument into something almost beatific.'

Let me now set straight my overall relationship with Bob Willis by observing with gratitude that his pithy unpredictable wit has enlivened many of our conversations on TV. As England's captain, he always came up trumps in this regard. It was a pleasure to have him join our TV commentary team, in which I think he now looks at affairs from a rather different stance.

For many years throughout the fifties and beyond, B.B.C. Television's basic cricket commentary team was composed of Brian Johnston, Jim Swanton and myself. We were joined regularly, after his playing career was done, by Denis Compton. Denis made his first TV broadcast in 1959, a summer when I missed a Test match on account of having mumps. 'We're very sorry Peter West isn't with us at the Oval,' Brian Johnston observed, 'and we hope all his troubles are small ones.'

Those were the days when 'talking faces' were acceptable: Jim and I alternated with our summaries in vision at close of play. These were often given with spectators crowding round the cameras, a distraction which Jim with imperious gestures sometimes sought to mitigate. In full flow he did not always take kindly to a signal from the stage manager that he should wind things up.

I rate Jim Swanton as the best summarizer of a day's play at a cricket match that I have seen or heard: a generous, ever-helpful colleague, somewhat larger than life, whose leg we delighted to pull. On one occasion at a Trent Bridge Test, Denis Compton contrived to have put out on the public address system a plea to Jim's chauffeur that he return at once to the car park because he had left his engine running. On another (which has been described by Brian Johnston in one of his bestselling books but can, I think, bear re-telling), a deep-laid scheme was devised at Canterbury in 1963 which required the cooperation of one of the umpires, Bill Copson, and Peter Richardson, a renowned practical joker whose achievements had included the printing of a Nottingham scorecard with a wholly fictitious Kent batting order. A handkerchief was waved from the TV commentary point above the sightscreen at Canterbury to indicate when Jim Swanton had taken over the microphone. Shortly after this signal was received Peter Richardson, opening the innings for Kent, was seen to be talking to Bill Copson and making gestures in the direction of our box. Copson then walked to the boundary edge below us and, keeping a remarkably straight face, said: 'The batsman is complaining that the booming noise coming from television is distracting him.' Colin Cowdrey, who was with us in the commentary box (having broken a wrist in the Lord's Test against the West Indies), cupped a hand to his ear. 'Can't hear you, Bill,' he said. 'Can you speak up?' To hear Jim Swanton talk his way through this little episode gave much delight to all concerned.

I had the pleasure of a rewarding televised chat with Jim in 1984, having first run him to earth in the M.C.C. committee box at Lord's. 'I interviewed the Archbishop of Canterbury yesterday,' I said. 'I can only follow that with you or the Pope.'

I submit a further tale about one of the most distinguished of all cricket reporters. In the days when Jim was also writing with discerning judgement about rugby for the *Daily Telegraph*, our paths crossed at Iffley Road where Oxford University were playing their annual match against Stanley's XV. There are some dozen seats reserved at the front of the stand, with a shelf provided for the scribes to take notes and compose their reports.

These were all occupied when the great man arrived to search for somewhere to park his ample presence. Gerard Walter of the old *News Chronicle* was sitting in one of the favoured positions. Fixing his monocle in one eye he turned round to enquire: 'Is anything worrying you, Jim? You look bothered.' 'Well, yes, I am,' Jim confided. 'I *would* like to be able to write.' 'Couldn't agree with you more, Jim,' Gerard Walter asserted. 'I've been reading your stuff for years.' Collapse of all parties in the press box.

Bryan Cowgill's arrival as TV's head of sport in the sixties brought radical changes in the cricket team. He decided the time was ripe for all commentary, running and otherwise, to be done by former Test cricketers, and I was lucky to be reprieved with a new role as presenter and interviewer. It offered new challenges, and I remain grateful to Bryan Cowgill for keeping me on board.

But Denis Compton became one of the casualties. It was held, I think, that as an interpolator he did not consistently provide the thoughtful analysis required. Denis, of course, was one of those marvellously gifted players who never had to think profoundly about the game. Without need for a net, he could rise from his slumbers in the dressing room, pick

97

up someone else's bat and go out to make a brilliant hundred. Everything came naturally to this instinctive genius. As one of Britain's great sporting heroes, Denis, throughout his years on television, retained a large and loyal following. Both he and Brian Johnston were the greatest fun to work with, and I was very sorry to see them depart the scene. I do not think either of them has forgiven television for the manner of their going. Both apparently were dropped from the team without a letter of explanation or thanks from the hierarchy for their services. A woeful illustration of declining standards.

Of Denis Compton's many shining virtues, a consistent punctuality on business or social occasions cannot be listed as one. In his commentating days it could never be assumed that he would be on time for the first broadcast after the lunch interval – perhaps on account of more pressing business with his bookmaker. There came a day when our producer, Phil Lewis, devised a little ploy to get his own back. When 'Compo' returned somewhat late to the commentary box, a stage manager, by arrangement with Phil Lewis, immediately informed him that the editor of 'Grandstand' in London required an immediate three-minute summary of the morning's play. In driving rain our chastened hero mounted a perpendicular ladder to the 'in-vision' position at Trent Bridge, was sat down in front of a camera, and at once cued – no umbrella apparently being available – to voice his thoughts. Two thirds of his way through them a drenched victim was given a pair of head phones so that he could hear his producer talking. 'I'd just like you to know, Denis,' Phil Lewis blithely announced, 'that you haven't been live on "Grandstand". We haven't even recorded it. But I thought you did very well in testing circumstances.'

Few would dispute that the B.B.C. got it right when uniting Richie Benaud and Jim Laker as a regular commentary duo. Richie first broadcast with radio in 1960, and with television in 1963. Jim made his TV debut on Sunday cricket and was first paired with Richie on B.B.C. 1 in 1968. To their immense knowledge and always perceptive comments Richie and Jim add total unflappability even in the hairiest of crises. Richie's calm and versatility are such that he seems able, at one and the same time, to give his attention to the game in hand, a study of *Sporting Life*, press articles for home and overseas consumption, broadcast scripts for Australia and any golf or racing that happens to be visible on a spare screen. His impartiality is unquestioned. He measures his judgements, remembering no doubt what a hard game it can be to play. He has a happy knack of being able to criticize without giving offence – even in the England dressing room where there have been some sensitive souls in recent years. His experience as one of cricket's outstanding leaders gives him an invaluable insight when assessing what captains are thinking – or at least what they should be thinking.

I have always thought that Jim Laker, with his wry, laconic sense of humour and an anecdote about almost every game in which he played, should lighten the winter of a cricketer's discontent with hours of reminiscence on the box. His down to earth approach as a commentator is one of utter honesty, and he has some vigorous views on what is happening, or ought to be happening, out in the middle. These have not always endeared him to some of England's leading players who may have supposed that anyone past the age of forty is out of touch with modern developments. Nonetheless, some trenchant views have needed to be aired in recent years, and we are all paid to say what we think. Not least someone who arguably is the greatest off-spinner of them all.

In front of a camera Jim does not invariably look as relaxed as he sounds behind his microphone in the commentary box, yet he frequently enlivens discussion with off-beat remarks which can be very funny indeed. Richie, his lips barely seen to move (he might have been a ventriloquist), takes everything in his impassive stride and woe betide the wretched interlocutor if a stupid question is posed. He doesn't suffer fools gladly.

Jim Laker's habit of droppin' his g's will not have escaped

general notice, and I am sure he will forgive me for quoting the following poem sent me, 'for whilin' away a rain break,' from Mr Jack Cookson in Walsall in 1976.

Negative 'G', or Jim Laker's Lament

The great day is dawnin'
For durin' the mornin'
The quest for the Ashes will start
With Jim commentatin'
And teams concentratin'
The nation's at least in good heart.

The English first innin's
From slow, sure beginnin's
Is takin' a turn for the worse,
The wickets are tumblin'
Supporters are grumblin'
The captain should be in a hearse.

How brittle our battin'
On grass or on mattin'
Tail-enders to rescue – take heart!
Why not send for Virgin
He'll need little urgin'
To tear the quick bowlers apart.

What with Roberts and Holdin'
And Holder, their bowlin'
Is more than we English can stand.
Excuses aren't heeded
No alibis needed
We're bein' emphatically tanned!

One of the expert interpolators, Tom Graveney, chats away in front of a camera as if to the manner born. His love of the game and his enthusiasm for the job simply glow through the screen. In an interview twosome his unfailing flexibility and professionalism are comforting for an anchorman needing to spread things out or bring down the curtain in a hurry. Tom, I might add, has a splendid method for dealing with correspondents who send him abusive letters. He replies with a get well card – unstamped.

Ted Dexter's forte is surely his expertise on technique and, so far as batsmanship is concerned, his insistence that it be governed by old-fashioned but still essential principles. He has an original, stimulating approach, and these days looks far happier in front of a camera than he sometimes did. There have been times when he could look somewhat distrait – so much so that several viewers of my acquaintance were convinced the Lord Edward had been the worse for alcoholic wear. I was able to reassure them that Ted, on broadcasting duty, has been a man of most abstemious habit.

At most of the big televised games these days interviews can be conducted under cover from the elements. But there have been occasions, much enjoyed by customers at the receiving end, when umbrellas in the great outdoors have not been proof against our fickle climate. On one such day at Edgbaston, His Lordship happened to remark to me that a nasty twinge down his umbrella handle indicated that he had been struck by lightning. Thinking this to be a light-hearted aside I callously ignored his remark and pressed on with another question. But he wasn't joking.

Nor was Richie Benaud, at Edgbaston again, when his protection against a sudden rain squall proved hopelessly inadequate. Exposed on the windward side, and receiving in his lap most of the water that fell from my umbrella, too, the Beau Brummell of our commentary box, always impeccably turned out, forced a distinctly wintry, tight-lipped smile. I treasure the memory of it.

Ray Illingworth was invited to join the television cricket team after despairingly throwing in his hand with Yorkshire at the end of the 1983 season. The B.B.C. knew just how good he was in a television role from the occasional contributions he had made during his playing career. Raymond missed no tactical tricks in his days as an outstanding captain, and he misses no nuances in a different capacity now. He shares with Jim Laker a Yorkshireman's belief that a spade should be called a bloody shovel, and airs it with a conviction not born of self-doubt.

Tony Lewis, a polished, articulate broadcaster (and journalist), is yet another member of the TV team on B.B.C. 1 whose experience of captaincy (with Cambridge University, Glamorgan, and England – in India in 1972) stands him in good stead. His versatility enables him to wear a variety of hats, whether as commentator, interpolator or anchorman. Tony may be asked to introduce most of the televised cricket in 1987, although as *Sunday Telegraph* cricket correspondent he would find it hard to serve two masters on a Saturday. Alternatively, it could be Peter Walker, another Glamorgan and England cricketer, who has been long established as a relaxed and highly professional broadcaster. I believe this workaholic is rarely off the air in Wales – in one medium or the other.

In recent summers Jack Bannister has sometimes joined the team. He has all the best qualities of a knowing old county professional, and his quietly perceptive comments (on radio as well as TV) are highly regarded by the cricketing fraternity. For many years now he has been a pillar of the Professional Cricketers' Association. The game stands in his debt for the measured and moderate way in which he has influenced and guided their policies, whether as chairman, treasurer or secretary.

Mike (M. J. K.) Smith made some forceful, always constructive comments in the seventies. I was sorry when he was dropped from our team. In recent seasons, when the Australians have toured here, we had some characteristically trenchant thoughts from Ian Chappell. This outstanding batsman and captain has an abrasive reputation but I believe in taking people as I find them. In his captaincy days he was unfailingly amenable and cooperative with television. In the commentary box he proved himself to be a genuine, even-tempered professional.

Ian Chappell has been one of Channel 9's regular cricket commentators in Australia. So has Tony Greig, whom I found it hard to forgive for his part – as England's captain – in the Packer affair. However, when he joined the B.B.C. team for coverage of the 1983 World Cup he was a delight to work with and – whether or not one agreed with everything he said – there could be no doubts about his all-round mastery of a new profession.

It is possible to televise a cricket match with two cameras, however basic and unsatisfying the coverage would be when judged by modern standards. Antony Craxton had only three of them when he took charge of B.B.C. televised cricket in the early fifties but, needless to say, had many more when directing, with much distinction, coverage of the big State occasions in his time. In those days cameras had fixed lenses which were rotated to change perspective. Zoom lenses, telerecordings and replays were all in the future then.

When England met Australia in 1985 our producer, Nick Hunter, had seven cameras at his disposal together with other items of gadgetry and hardware. Camera 1, ideally installed fifteen to twenty feet above the ground, is lined up middle stump to middle stump. It takes the master shot to which the producer 'cuts' just before the ball is delivered, and it remains virtually fixed while the batsmen take their runs and the ball is returned to the wicketkeeper. When you see the fielder in action, the shot from camera 1 is sometimes inlaid in a top corner of the screen: an idea first used by Channel 9 in Australia.

Hard by camera 1, and usually on its left hand side, number 2 follows the ball's delivery on a wider-angled shot. If the angle is tightened too close, the speed of an edged stroke to a fielder may well leave the camera behind. A full-blooded stroke to gully requires a lightning reaction from the producer as he cuts from one camera to another. It will be seen that if camera 2 fails to discover where the ball has gone, meaningful coverage is hard to sustain – and sometimes the ball goes to unlikely places. A producer ensures if he can that camera 2 is operated by someone who has played cricket and knows which direction the nicks and top edges may take.

Camera 3 is placed at ground level to the left of the sight-screen. This offers a close-up of batsman or bowler and, with any luck, another close-up of the catcher at *le moment critique*. If the cameraman is really adept, he might even provide a picture of slips or wicketkeeper at such a moment. Dexterity and anticipation are the names of his game, and here again it is clearly not a job for Tom, Dick or Harry weaned on fixed shots in the comfort of a studio. His ability to identify all the players is an added advantage. In the last few years the output from camera 3 has been fed to its own recording machine, known as a VPR, which can be used in slow motion – a relatively new development even though video tapes have been long available.

Building up coverage from left of centre, camera 4, also at ground level, is stationed at mid-wicket. This one does not follow the ball but concentrates on the players, the umpires and the crowd to get their reactions. Its routine shots dwell on batsman or bowler, and it often pans with the bowler during his walk back. Providing some useful slow motion of a bowler's approach and delivery from sideways on, it is regarded as a vital camera for a Test match but not so crucial for lesser encounters.

Why is the television coverage mounted from left of centre? The B.B.C. believes that in this fashion they provide the best seat or seats in the ground, but it is important that one position is related to the other so that viewers are not left restless and disorientated. They have become accustomed to the coverage, have only a hazy notion of where the cameras are, but are happy to take them for granted. When, at a John Player League game on a Sunday, the mid-wicket camera shot pictures from the opposite (right) side of the ground, the pattern was broken and it was difficult to know which end was which.

Camera 5, hoisted by crane to a suitable height, takes reverse angle shots from the far end. It is never used live. During alternate overs its output is fed into the VPR machine already mentioned. Ideally it would go to another machine: in a perfect world the B.B.C. producer would have two cameras at the far end to mirror those behind the wicket at the nearer one. But the B.B.C.'s considerable camera resources are stretched to cover a wide variety of outside events in the summer. Australia's Channel 9 has no such problems. Yet camera 5 provides some ideal replays of lbw's seen more clearly from the distant end.

Camera 6 is used for interviews as well as shots of the scoreboard and crowds. At Headingley or Old Trafford, where the pavilion is square-on to the pitch, the players have a longish walk to the 'studio' point, perhaps in bad weather and almost certainly pursued by autograph hunters. So on those grounds the B.B.C. provides a hand-held camera, and the mountain goes to Mahomet.

For Cornhill Test matches as well as for the Benson and Hedges and Nat West Cup finals at Lord's, a seventh camera is installed high at mid-wicket (still on the left hand side) to provide not only a fresh angle on the fielding but, in slow motion, conclusive proof one way or the other about a run-out. This confirms, much more often than not, the accurate judgement of an umpire faced with a split-second decision, but with no replay to help him. It can do the same for stumpings. But the most sophisticated camera coverage in the world will never prove whether an lbw decision is right or wrong. That must remain a matter of opinion.

Kerry Packer's Channel 9 in Australia proceeds on the same basic principles as the B.B.C. but duplicates coverage from both ends, using far more hardware, and projects the cricket with the bowler always running away from the camera, regardless of the end from which he is operating. I am probably in a minority these days in preferring the old conventional coverage of the B.B.C. I find the Australian method disorientating: it is difficult to tell which end is which. But I have to concede that many viewers hardly seem to notice the difference.

As to Channel 9's hardware, David Hill, their resourceful and imaginative producer, was never observed by Nick Hunter to have less than nine cameras at his disposal and for one day and night match in Sydney he had thirteen. One of these, in a helicopter, and another, high on a flood-lighting tower, provided some spectacular shots.

Whereas in recent years the B.B.C. has had one VPR recording machine (two for Tests and Cup Finals), Channel 9 has had anything between four and six. This means that while the B.B.C. may have struggled to achieve the best-angled replay, Australian coverage has had no such problems – even though we may have needed to watch several angles before it found the right one. All this Australian hardware makes the direction of cameras and recording machines a distinctly complicated matter. Remarkably enough, Brian Morelli of Channel 9 does this job on his own. But he has a vision mixer to help him, and he gets a respite when the commercials are screened. Morelli's expertise has left David Hill to concentrate exclusively on masterminding the coverage as editor. Hill spends most of his day directing operations from a plush commentary box.

Another important difference between B.B.C. and Channel 9 coverage lies in Australian ability to retain the same specialist cameramen throughout a summer. I am not denigrating the skills of B.B.C. cameramen versatile enough to turn their hand to every kind of outside broadcast. But the advantages of having an unchanged team working on cricket coverage must be evident, and to cover the 1985 Cornhill series against Australia, Nick Hunter, for the first time, had four cameramen on regular duty. This was a distinct acquisition of strength, and it was reflected in the end-product. I am suggesting there is nothing Australian production achieves which could not be equalled or bettered by the B.B.C.'s Nick Hunter with one regular camera team and the same amount of hardware. Technical coverage of the last Australian series here was – as Michael Grade, Controller of B.B.C. 1, asserted – a brilliant affair. The Somerset cricketer Peter Roebuck clearly took a different view when writing in *The Guardian* in 1985. He found B.B.C. coverage stodgy and lethargic, catering only for the connoisseur. I might say the same thing about his batting.

Hardware apart, the *style* of coverage is different in England and Australia. Australian camera-work is more aggressive. Australian commentators talk more – partly because they have no chance to say anything between the overs or at the fall of a wicket, when commercials are screened. But the Australian cricket public likes more chat. Whenever B.B.C. cricket has been screened direct to the other side of the world, there were frequent requests from the southern hemisphere for more talk. Richie Benaud, working for both channels in his all but perpetual summer, contrives to satisfy the customers in two hemispheres. I trust we will never see the day when the B.B.C. apes Channel 9 by superimposing on their screens a Walt Disney-like character such as Daddles the duck. It may be adored by the kids in Australia but it has not been top of the pops in the players' dressing rooms.

These days it is taken for granted both in England and Australia that computerized scores and statistics will embroider the output. Thirty years ago viewers in these islands were content with a regular shot of the scoreboard and verbal comment during an over while runs accrued or wickets fell. By the sixties B.B.C. Television had acquired the services of Maurice Ryman who maintained – with an inevitable time lag – a scoresheet in handsome copperplate handwriting. It all seemed quite swish and stylish at the time. By the end of the last decade, thanks to the initiative of

Ted Dexter, televised cricket had entered the computerized era.

Dexter arranged talks between the B.B.C. and one of the big computer firms, Honeywell. After lengthy experiment, and some trial and error, the B.B.C. had an exciting, versatile new piece of gadgetry to provide an automatic update on every run scored and every ball bowled. The computer gives up-to-the-second analyses of batsmen's and bowlers' performances not just in the match being played but over their careers as a whole. When a cricketer achieves a 'best performance', the computer signals it instantaneously. All this as a result of the scorer, before each game, providing essential information which is fed into the machine by a four-man computer/caption team expertly led by Peter Pickering. Nick Hunter will not deny that after so much effort had been expended in the production of this facility there was a temptation to over-use it. Statistics, it is said, can prove anything. But boring, unimportant ones can switch viewers off.

Cricket statisticians are an interesting breed, in that many of them are more concerned with figures than the arts and graces of the game. Two of the scorers for B.B.C. Television, Roy Webber, and the cricket historian, Irving Rosenwater, must be included in this category. I hasten to add that both, in their different styles, did an extremely efficient scoring job. It is a hard one demanding unremitting concentration for six hours or more a day, not to mention all the time required for research and for keeping their information up to date. Roy Webber died of a heart attack, as did his successor in the commentary box, Jack Price. Another scorer, Michael Fordham, who married Roy Webber's widow, Daphne, and worked with us on those occasions when more than one match was being televised, passed on when still in his pomp. Ross Salmon, who succeeded Jack Price for several years, survived a serious car accident.

Since Irving Rosenwater went out to Australia some years ago to work for Channel 9, and then to settle there, the

B.B.C.'s television scorer has been Wendy Wimbush. Maintaining the standards set by her male predecessors, she makes an inconspicuous yet vital contribution to the operation. Unlike radio, in which the commentator is virtual king, television is only as good as the sum of its many component parts.

When listing the names of those scorers no longer with us I should have added that of Arthur Wrigley, who died after working with B.B.C. Radio in the post-war years. A leg spinner who had been good enough to join Lancashire's staff at Old Trafford before the war, he added to his command of facts and figures a profound knowledge of the game. If a commentator happened to miss seeing a dismissal or a dropped catch, Arthur could be relied on to fill him in with an accurate report of the incident (I could not say the same of everyone else in his trade). The immensely efficient Bill Frindall, with whom I have worked only rarely, tirelessly performs just as reliable a service for his radio colleagues on Test Match Special.

Two of my cricket producers, Philip Lewis and Nick Hunter, have played a prime part in the boom which snooker now enjoys. Convinced that the game would have a future on colour television, Philip Lewis created 'Pot Black' for the screen. In recent years Nick Hunter's conviction that championship snooker transmitted at length – and not just in an edited half-hour chunk at midnight – would attract and hold vast audiences, has been triumphantly vindicated. The skills and sportsmanship of the players no doubt have had a lot to do with that. The game's infinite variety has surely been a telling factor, too. No two frames of snooker can ever be the same.

On a melancholy note, I recall with sadness that two of our most respected cricket producers have also passed on. David Kenning, who was in executive charge of the output for eight years in the seventies, died in a London hospital in 1983 when making what appeared to be a good recovery after a car crash on a holiday in Spain. He was not always easy to work with but he had a brilliant talent, including the shrewdest editorial sense, which he applied to the coverage of a variety of sports. Bill Taylor died of cancer in 1985 after a long illness most courageously borne. I was touched to be asked, as was Bill McLaren, too, to act as one of the pall-bearers at his funeral. Bill Taylor, a devoted family man, loved his rugby and his cricket. He was a very experienced, utterly reliable old pro who had been a stage manager and cameraman, and knew his craft from A to Z. Above all, this staunchest of Scots was ever a loyal and honest friend.

Some may think the word professional is over-used in this book, but I know of no other which so simply encapsulates a man's determination to do his job to the best of his capacity and to an established criterion of quality. Without apology I shall now use it again, and I am mindful of the fact that in an era of declining standards in many aspects of life, the B.B.C.'s televised sport has never been in business to finish second. I count myself lucky to have worked for many years at the cricket with so professional, disciplined and happy a team – in production, commentary and every aspect involved in keeping the show on the road. The talk needs to be apposite since the picture exerts its own discipline at every moment of the day. A genial atmosphere is important when working in harness for many hours on end. There's no place for prima donnas.

As one of the very few who has regularly presented himself on television with a 'short back and sides' but decreasing thatch on top, I long ago came to the conclusion that I could not stop my hair falling out yet might hope to limit the number of chins and contain an expanding waistline. I never stooped to the indignity of acquiring the toupee so often advised by ruder friends, but most of us with a few strands of hair on a balding pate prefer to be portrayed by the cameras in the kindliest light. Whereas in a sizeable, indoor studio the lighting arrangements are usually made with flattering care, those on outside sporting occasions – frequently in confined and testing circumstances – tend to be put together in perfunctory fashion. The lights are often too high, too hot and too harsh. Only a handful of the many estimable producers and production managers within my experience has evinced any obvious interest in the matter.

I have been asked by viewers on many occasions whether make-up girls were available to ameliorate the ravages of time. At Wimbledon, yes, though in saying that I imply no disrespect to Harry Carpenter for whom a touch of powder on forehead and nose is enough to enhance a noble image. At the cricket, as sometimes in my case would have been obvious enough, the answer is no. 'I saw the old man on telly,' the butcher confides to one's better half next day. 'Is he all right?' Give me, any time, the natural light of the great outdoors.

It remains an occasional comfort to be assured by viewers met for the first time that you look better 'in real life'. A good deal more acceptable, indeed, than a comment I heard once: 'Ye gods, you look a bloody sight better on the box.' Or even another observation: 'Well, we heard what you said on TV. Now tell us what you really think.'

I have never ceased to be surprised by the things viewers write about, and cricket has provided my files with many interesting samples. One particular subject has sparked off a steady flow, and I quote some examples of it: 'I take the liberty of asking you to help stop the vulgar practice of our fast bowlers polishing the ball down their middles. I often change over to the sound radio to escape my view of such a filthy habit.'

A Mr Windle in Chelmsford wrote: 'I do not profess to understand cricket because I never had the chance to play much. But I should like to know why bowlers when they walk back facing the camera are always scratching their balls. I can't think why and it's very rude.'

'Can you please tell me,' enquired a viewer in St Andrews, Fife, 'if the camera crew take a special delight in showing the bowlers polishing the ball about their privates? We are keen enthusiasts but the female side of the family have to leave the viewing in disgust.'

A Lt-Col Watts, Retired, adjured us, from Harpole in Northants, to break ourselves of the habit of talking about a ball bowled as a delivery. 'Women have deliveries,' he thundered. 'Bowlers have balls.'

A viewer in Scarborough said he felt obliged to comment on the performance of a commentary team 'which seems likely soon to outnumber the protagonists themselves.' He went on to remark that Richie Benaud's twang was just about the most grating thing on TV. 'In particular I wish he would get away from "deliveries" and simply say "balls", as I frequently do when I'm listening to him.'

My special favourite came from the King's Road, Chelsea in 1963. 'Why on Friday did Tony Lock keep interfering with his trousers and holding his crutch? Evidently good manners and a little breeding are lacking. I wondered maybe if the Jew boys Johnston, Compton, Dexter and Trueman conveyed him to the local synagogue and had him circumcised.'

'Dear babbling brook,' was the unpromising form of address on a post card from Ipswich in the sixties. 'What an old woman you are. Take a leaf out of R. Benaud's book: a fine man and a great cricketer. I suggest you team up with Godfrey Winn and do a season with the Women's Institutes.' From the Barracks at Norton in Worcestershire, signed by 'many viewers', came another complaint: 'We do wish you would not speak so close to the mike on TV. Every time you say "six" and "slips" it makes you sound like a sissie. The same applies to Jack Fingleton, who whistles through his dentures.' Jack, whose writing on the game was so unfailingly readable and entertaining, enjoyed that one too. He contributed much wit and wisdom to TV and radio commentaries before falling out – I never quite discovered how or why – with an influential hierarch at Broadcasting House. After that I was still able, whenever the Australians toured here, to snaffle him for a televised chat during an interval or a rain break. Anyone interviewing Jack needed to be on the *qui vive*: it was a stimulating experience. A rich character of whom I was very fond, he did not care for some of the modern trends in Test cricket and was never reluctant to speak his mind.

Just as I discovered how dangerous it is for a Sassenach to comment on anything pertaining to the Scots, so I learned to be wary of Yorkshiremen when talking about their cricketing heroes. My education began early. 'Your remarks on the present Test,' announced a letter from the Dales, 'are absolutely disgusting and if you had any sense of decency you would resign.' And here is another sample: 'When Trueman was playing your sense of fair play was lacking. Any carping criticism you could make you certainly did, and you are at it again with Hutton and Wardle. I am writing to the B.B.C. about you and I am not by myself in this respect. I hope you are not an Englishman but if by some mischance you are then for God's sake go. If you cannot be fair, then don't be dirty.' My anonymous correspondent failed to put a stamp on the envelope and I had to pay double to read the damned thing.

I had to admire the conviction of another correspondent who accused me in 1985 of 'typical Southern bias' against Arnie Sidebottom and then, submitting his XII for the next encounter against Australia, managed to include only seven Yorkshiremen in the list. And that, believe it or not, didn't include the name of Geoff Boycott. No one, I think, is more knowledgeable about the game of cricket than the genuine, dyed-in-the-wool Yorkshire supporter. Yet it is a myth that the general Yorkshire public possesses a more instinctive feel for its finer points than those elsewhere. The same applies in my own county of Kent where you can hear as much rubbish talked about cricket – some of it in the member's enclosures – as you will in most other places. The difference, as the Boycott saga has illustrated, is that Yorkshire folk will leap to a prickly defence of their heroes.

This is exactly what they did in 1967 when the Yorkshire

and England captain, Brian Close, created a stir in a county championship match at Edgbaston by using delaying tactics which, in the opinion of the leading reporters present, flouted the spirit of the game. John Woodcock in *The Times* and Michael Melford in the *Daily Telegraph* both condemned the tactics in outspoken fashion. Now if it be held that this southerner, not himself present at Edgbaston, was influenced by the establishment press, let him add that Jim Kilburn, respected correspondent of the *Yorkshire Post*, took an equally sour view of what he had seen his county captain doing. Not long afterwards I had a similar report from the Yorkshire scorer (and former opening batsman), Ted Lester, who admitted that the whole business had left him feeling mightily embarrassed.

The wires hummed, the presses buzzed, the cricketing hierarchy closeted itself in secret conclave, and in due course I found myself with a big story on my hands. I learned that as a result of the Edgbaston affair Brian Close was to be deposed from the England captaincy and that Colin Cowdrey was to replace him as leader of the M.C.C. team due to tour the West Indies the following winter. Resisting the temptation to sell the story to a popular newspaper for a substantial reward, I offered it instead to B.B.C. Television. It is not every day of the week that TV scoops Fleet Street on a major sporting topic. The B.B.C. were grateful for this opportunity but understandably concerned, if they were to nail their colours to the mast, that I had got the facts right. The head of sport, Bryan Cowgill – a newsman to his cuticles – and the editor of 'Sportsview', Alan Hart – another hungry journalist – must have kept their fingers crossed. I did, too. Might there have been, at the eleventh hour, a change of heart, a change of plan at Lord's?

Cowgill and Hart decided that I should present the news as a reporter, leaving others to make the comment. It did not surprise me on arriving at the 'Sportsview' studio to hear that a well-known Yorkshire journalist, Michael Parkinson (in those days not the accomplished television chat show host he later became) had accepted an invitation to state some predictable views. In the meantime the B.B.C. were seeking to 'balance' the projected discussion by finding someone south of the Trent to present a different slant. Denis Compton, Ted Dexter and David Sheppard, then Bishop of Woolwich, were approached, but none of them was available at short notice. Eventually the B.B.C. ran out of time and ideas. So this news reporter, offered the hot seat opposite the Barnsley terror, came to wish with the benefit of hindsight that he had had the sense to decline it.

Parkinson's law on this matter would have been taken for granted by anyone familiar with his cricket writings in the *Sunday Times*. These, when he sought to amuse, were invariably a most diverting read. But when he wrote seriously about the first-class game, it appeared that Yorkshire players could do no wrong and that a blimpish incompetent hierarchy at Lord's, traditionally prejudiced in favour of the old school tie, could do no right. It was Colin Cowdrey's misfortune that, however modestly he wore one, he could not conceal or disclaim his background.

Parkinson upheld the actions of Close at Edgbaston as being totally justifiable. He maintained that criticism of them had been whipped up by a southern press coterie hand in glove with the so-called cricket establishment. Winning was the name of the game: the end justified the means. English cricket needed winners; a strong, positive leader such as Close. Cowdrey was negative, a southern softie. The faceless ones of Lord's had leapt at an opportunity to restore an amateur captain at the expense of a hardened professional.

I said that I had always respected Close as a brave and resourceful cricketer, as a forceful captain, but it would be a sorry thing if what he had done at Edgbaston was now to be regarded as an acceptable part of the game. I suggested that if he had apologized for it, if he had admitted that he had allowed his zeal to outrun his judgement, he might well have remained as England's captain. A stubbornness that often served him well on the cricket field had not allowed him to swallow his pride.

I may not have suffered a knock-down but I certainly lost the contest on points. Next morning the press climbed aboard, and in no time at all the age-old north-south controversy had been whipped into flame. A day or so later I set off to Harrogate, there to report for *The Times* a contest between Yorkshire and Gloucestershire, the result of which was crucial to Yorkshire's hopes of winning the county championship. Little did I think on entering the ground that I was about to bring a county match to a temporary halt.

The booing and catcalling began as soon as I had turned inside the gates and made my way in front of the stand. Halfway through the day's first over, Gloucestershire's Tony Brown stopped in the middle of his run-up and all the players looked to see what the commotion was about. I had a quick decision to make: whether to beat a prudent retreat or to keep going, the pavilion in my sights, and sweat it out. I rejected the spineless course and pressed on regardless. It was not a pleasant experience. The pavilion seemed a long way off, and the booing went on until I got there.

On the Yorkshire team balcony the players were enjoying the joke while this itinerant commentator ran the gauntlet. It struck me that I might still find some friends in their dressing room, in spite of what had occurred on 'Sportsview'. Head bloodied but unbowed, I found temporary refuge with Brian Close and his men. 'Bowled Parky for nowt,' the captain said with the broadest of grins and not the slightest sign of malice. But, alas, the more hostile of the natives were not disposed to forgive. For three days on that Harrogate ground I suffered abuse wherever I went.

When I got home again, the letters had started to arrive via the B.B.C. 'You are a snob, a hypocrite, a humbug and a stuffed shirt.' 'May I wish you, Colin Cowdrey and his pals at the M.C.C. every discomfort as the touring team gets thrashed in the West Indies this winter.' (England, thanks admittedly to a generous declaration by Gary Sobers, won the series 2-1). 'You, Compton and the rest of the M.C.C. snobs must be feeling sick tonight. Yorkshire are champions. Cowdrey no doubt was afraid to turn up at Scarborough but of course he always was a yellow-belly.' Well, I never saw Cowdrey flinch even when facing the fastest of bowling. He even managed to appear calm when, during his next visit to Headingley, a hooligan scratched the paint on his new car from bonnet to boot.

It is pleasant to reflect that when I next went to Harrogate, a season or two later, all was sweetness and light. But the echoes of that 'Sportsview' episode lasted longer than I supposed. Arriving for a Test match at Headingley, I was informed by a superintendent of police that I had to be provided with their protection during the match. They had received a letter, anonymous it need not be said, from a friendly soul in Goole. 'We beg to inform you,' it declared, 'that if Peter West comes to Leeds for the Test match, there is going to be trouble we are going to bash him we shall get him one way or the other it is no hoax he is hated all over Yorkshire and we intend to get at him and it will be as well if he does not come.' I survived unscathed. My official escort, a keen cricketer, rather enjoyed the assignment.

There is, of course, nothing special about the abusive mail received by commentators; players, notably captains when things are going badly, get their share of it as well. A former Kent and England skipper treasures a letter simply addressed to 'Denness, cricketer,' which reads, 'If this ever finds you the Post Office have a higher opinion of you than I have.'

Chapter Six

EARLY IN 1956 I WAS asked by Bill Duncalf, then one of the senior producers in Outside Broadcasts, to join the B.B.C.'s commentary team at Wimbledon. Absorbed by cricket at school, I had indulged in a little social tennis of derisory standard but was confident I had an essential 'feel' for anything played with a ball. It was a challenging assignment because I had to uproot myself from cricket, which occupied much of my summer, and overnight take up station on No. 1 court in a totally different environment.

On the first day or two of the championships – until I had found fresh bearings – I had to beware of slipping in a familiar cricket expression. This self-discipline, alas, did not save me on a later occasion from observing that Nancy Richey, resplendent in her old-fashioned Bermuda shorts, had worn them ever since she was a boy. Nor, later still, from describing Jan Kodes, after four stamina-sapping sets, as coming up fresh as a pansy for the last one. Nor even, at another time, from seeking to describe an Argentine doubles combination as a pair of shrewd and crafty players, but perpetrating an unfortunate Spoonerism instead. I admit to saying that Betty Stove had gone off the boil. I confess authorship of a remark that another lady player would be sure to pull something out in a crisis. But it was not me who said that Rod Laver was about to serve from the new box end with the royal balls.

Television at Wimbledon in the mid-fifties, as compared with the present scene, had the air of a pleasant garden party. In that era there was no video tape, no slow motion, no replay. The day's recordings were processed overnight. Cameras, on both the big show courts, were installed at the royal box end facing a setting sun, and there was no visual coverage of action occurring elsewhere. The atmosphere was soon to change, first with the arrival of commercial television which was to cover Wimbledon for many years until it retired from the scene with unsatisfying viewing figures, then with the appointment of Bryan Cowgill to mastermind the B.B.C.'s effort as a highly demanding but intensely professional editor.

Cowgill, a workaholic of immense drive and ambition, maintained the new-found impetus at Wimbledon and in every other sporting activity on which he set his decisive imprint when he became Head of B.B.C. TV Sport. He often drove himself and his henchmen berserk: a perfectionist who needed to be judged by the quality of the end-product. The time has long gone since B.B.C. TV Sport could afford to be complacent about the quality of the opposition's product, I.T.V.'s coverage of soccer and racing being two notable examples of that truth. Cowgill's reign at Wimbledon ensured there was no complacency in those days either. He brought to his task a newsman's editorial flair, he chiselled away at the All England Club in his search for new camera positions and facilities, and he transformed what was already by contemporary standards a respected professional operation into something that was not in business to finish second best.

Not everyone concurred about the merits of Cowgill's editorial judgements. I received a postcard, addressed to the B.B.C. Outfit and ominously datemarked from Muckrush Heath in Dorset, which read as follows: 'Everyone connected with transmitting Wimbledon for the B.B.C. is AN ULTRA-MORONIC SPECIES OF PUBLIC PLAGUE. There was NO excuse for handing over in a typically mentally

constipated way to the Centre Court match . . . If you were
not malevolents OR morons (or both) you would realize that
your ELEMENTARY DUTY is to give viewers a CONSPEC-
TUS of everything of main interest. If you can't do this you
should pack it in and apply for jobs as ball boys.'

At times when the tennis was transmitted on only one
channel an editor – like the wretched commentators – could
never hope to please all of the people all of the time. For
much of the play the B.B.C. is now able to offer viewers a
choice and the best of both worlds, on B.B.C. 1 or 2. With
extra cameras, moreover, on outside courts the B.B.C. can
justly claim to cover 'all the important action'. In television
terms the direction of cameras at a tennis match is a good
deal less testing than, say, at cricket, golf or motor racing.
That is not to suggest that the overall Wimbledon coverage,
involving sixteen or seventeen cameras and an army of
technicians, is not a most complicated operation in its provision of the right pictures and the right sound at any given
moment. But in basic terms televising the game itself
implies having one 'master' camera at exactly the right
height and position to cover the rallies, with just minimal
movement one way or the other when the players run wide,
and two more providing close-ups of the protagonists. Extra
cameras, such as the one positioned behind the server or
receiver – which provides a vivid picture of the pace of the
ball – are the icing on the cake. So too is the replay facility
now so slickly inter-woven with the action, even between
points, that it is difficult to believe that tennis could be presented with greater polish.

A singles match on television is much easier to cover than
a doubles. Skilled directors, supported by flexible, fast-
reacting cameramen, can – for all but the cognoscenti – turn
a humdrum doubles encounter into something more
compelling than it really is. Interestingly enough, the player
who *loses* a point, in singles or doubles, usually reacts more
dramatically than the one who wins it.

When commentators are stuck in a hot, oppressively

sticky box for hours on end it can be relaxing to exchange an occasional quip with their directors on the 'talk back' microphone providing for conversation unheard by the public. This implies a need for the headset microphone to be, as it were, in the right gear. Forward, in top and you are speaking to the great big public. Neutral, and you can talk your head off with no one hearing a word save neighbours in the box. Back, in bottom gear, and you are in contact with your director. I defy any commentator to claim that he has got through a championship without finding himself in the wrong gear.

Words of supposed wisdom have not always found receptive ears. 'Why do commentators have to talk *all* the time,' one viewer asked, amidst a stream of other complaints. 'I speak, what's more, on behalf of thousands who cannot stand your ceaseless blather.' (They always do: perhaps he had taken a straw poll?) Another, more succinctly, said: 'I can't stand it any longer. FOR GOD'S SAKE, BELT UP.' And yet another enquired: 'Would it be painful for you to keep your six-inch aperture closed during tense moments?' Wimbledon commentators resent the suggestion that they talk *all* the time. It has always been a golden rule never to do so during the rallies. In his brief sojourn as Head of Outside Broadcasts (Television), S. J. de Lotbiniere set down a dictum which none of us should ever forget. 'A television commentator,' he decreed, 'earns his fee as much by silence as by speech.' In the years since then that custom has been honoured too often in the breach than the observance. I do not doubt I have breached it too often myself, but I must add that in cricket and tennis over the years there has been a greater discipline in this respect than in some other sports I can think of.

The doyen, Dan Maskell, has not escaped the blast. I had one letter which queried whether it was not high time that I, Mark Cox and Grandpa Daniel stopped waffling and talking drivel on the box. Another implored me not to chatter so much and not to emphasize the obvious like that ghastly bore Maskell. I dare say Dan would supply similar samples from his own mail if he had not thrown them straight into the waste paper basket or had them so disposed of by his senior producer before he was able to read them.

There have been times when I thought I could do *nothing* right, as the following extract may suggest: 'You are ruining my enjoyment again by your awful and revolting habit of *heavy breathing* into the mike when you're not talking. It makes me feel sick.' Or another: 'Will you please stop whispering and mumbling? You have not got good diction anyway. Speak up or shut up. Listen to Dan Maskell, then you may be fit to commentate next year.' And another: 'If you must keep up a perpetual burble may I request you are at least audible? A copy of this is going to your boss.'

We all have our prejudices, no doubt, though commentators are wise to subdue them in public. This does not save us from being charged with bias, ignorance, incompetence or plain distortion of what the customer regards as fact. After a match between Ann Jones and Virginia Wade a viewer in Plymstock, Devon wrote: 'Ann Jones loses a set and she's playing badly. She wins one and oh! she's a wonderful player. You are so ready to praise the top dog and undermine the loser. No glory is ever given to Ann. You should know by now that she likes to lose a set before she gets going.' There's news for you, Ann.

Institutions, even Dan Maskell, have never been immune to criticism. None of us is indispensable in this demanding world, but millions would declare that Wimbledon without him will never be the same. With his love and knowledge of tennis, his measured, articulate tones and almost life-long experience within the game, he brings to the annual ritual a special amalgam that can never be replaced. I have sometimes wondered with irreverence what Dan's reactions would be in the commentary box on the day – may it never arrive – when a streaker appears on the Centre Court or, a much less likely manifestation, when that sward is transformed into an artificial surface. It is a comfort to reflect that the All England Club intends to continue staging the greatest of tennis championships on grass. Dan wears marvellously well at the age of seventy-eight, and shows no inclination to retire.

For many years Dan Maskell's 'other half' in the Centre Court commentary box was Jack Kramer, who had been, in 1947, one of Wimbledon's outstanding champions. It was in many ways an unlikely alliance which worked a treat: Dan the English traditionalist and Jack the extroverted American who added relaxed, always wise and often salty comment. There were people who disliked Jack's accent and apparently resented the intrusion of an American into something they regarded as being an exclusively English preserve. I was never able to understand this chauvinistic attitude but the small minority which abhorred Kramer must have been satisfied when he became persona non grata at the All England Club. When most of the world's top players declined to play at Wimbledon in 1973, Kramer's espousal of the professionals' cause was something that stuck painfully in the club's gullet. With great regret and I am sure not a little heart-searching the B.B.C. decided not to renew his contract. In the years since then they have been unable to find anyone from overseas remotely in Jack's class as an interpolator.

The role of the interpolator is a very special and exacting one requiring not just expertise but an acute sense of timing so that their comments smoothly dovetail into the action. There were times on No. 1 Court when I found myself teamed with former players of distinction who would have known exactly what to do had they been out there with a racket in their hands, but were hard pushed in the commentary box to put their thoughts into succinct and acceptably accented words. Much more often, happily enough, I was associated with Bill Knight, an immensely gritty Davis Cup left-hander. The suggestion was made, and I do not doubt it's truth, that a combination of Knight's resilience and Bobby Wilson's skills, notably his backhand, might have produced a world champion. Whether it be true or not, Bill Knight brought to the commentary box a capacity, unrivalled in my experience, for explaining the tactics of a match, putting a knowing finger on the strengths and weaknesses of the players and pointing out what they were seeking, or ought to be seeking, to do. Sadly, in the midseventies, the B.B.C. let Bill Knight go. I suggest that someone in high authority did not like his sturdy Northampton accent. A progressive concern with running his family furniture business, which meant that he could not always be available for other commentaries, may have been a contributory factor.

When in 1967 the B.B.C.'s coverage of Wimbledon was first beamed across the Channel – oh! heady days – I was required to introduce the show in vision and thought it very exciting. When B.B.C. 2 first went on the air at the championships, extra cameras were installed at the other end of the Centre Court (where all of them now do duty), with Messrs Knight and West doing the commentary. We both remember the experience vividly, having taken up stations at a quarter to two, commentated on five matches spread over seven hours and being released from travail at 8.50 p.m. There were no spare commentators to bring relief for us – or for those viewers who heard two voices ad nauseam. By the end of it all we both felt whacked.

Some may suggest it ought to be a privilege to have a free seat on Centre Court, as indeed it is, but I invite those who have not had the experience of sitting cooped up in a tiny box, concentrating mind and eye alternately and in rapid sequence on the action and a monitor screen, *not* to feel tired by the effort after a few hours. Commentators, being human, are at their freshest in the early part of a transmission, and more prone to error later on, often when the audience is at its biggest in early evening. The B.B.C. hierarchy, long aware of this problem, now engages a larger team of commentators which ensures – in theory at least – that none of them will be worked into the ground. Dan Maskell has relished this relatively new arrangement, but try prising him away from the commentary box when one of his British lads or lasses takes play into the fourth hour and a final set.

The departure from the Wimbledon scene of Bill Knight provided further opportunities for John Barrett, a former British Davis Cup player and captain with whom I also spent many happy hours on No. 1 Court. Later, when Mark Cox's playing career was nearing its end, another British left-hander became regularly available to the B.B.C. Mark's quiet, telling and always thoughtful comments never seem to intrude on the action. John Barrett, a gifted all-rounder, has the versatility to fill the role of commentator or interpolator.

When I first worked at Wimbledon, all matches, whether men's or women's, were covered by male commentators. The B.B.C. subsequently persisted in a search for interpolators representing the fairer sex and some extremely well known champions suffered defeat in the commentary box. But Ann Jones, with her tactical expertise, was a much respected addition of strength in the seventies, and Virginia Wade later joined the team to establish a successful alternating duo for the women's game.

Throughout the seventies the senior B.B.C. producer or editor at Wimbledon was A. P. ('Slim') Wilkinson, a professional of ripe experience and unquestioned integrity who, following the end of the championships, would regularly take himself off to the Open golf where he performed a like service. Those were the days when I did most of the Wimbledon interviews. I had a love/hate relationship with Slim on those occasions when I was immersed in a splendid contest on court only to receive an urgent message to the effect that so-and-so was about to relieve me in the commentary box and would I therefore get myself at once to the interview room to talk with, say, Jimmy Connors after his match elsewhere? Swearing at Slim but silently relishing the challenge, I would pick up a few essential facts and figures on the way, and slip quietly into the press interview room – if I could get there in time – to hear what the player had to say there. Armed by all this information I could then confront my victim with more confidence.

I propound the theory that Americans are the easiest people in the world to interview, while the British can be the most introverted and difficult. Yet the readiness of Jimmy Connors to talk was less marked after I had interviewed him at the Wimbledon Centenary championships in 1977. We all know James to be a great competitor but on that occasion he had enraged Britain's tennis establishment as well as a much wider audience by refusing to join the parade of former champions. He practised on an outside court instead. I felt entitled when talking to him to take a firm line by reflecting the general view. Later in those championships he reached the semi-finals and I arrived in the interview room for another chat by way of hors d'oeuvre before his next encounter. 'I'm not,' Connors announced when he saw me, 'going to be interviewed by *that* guy.' A minor crisis was averted when Harry Carpenter was hurriedly summoned to take my place. Harry is one of the great television professionals, a man who has introduced and linked the Wimbledon output for almost twenty years, remaining as modest and as easy to work with as he was when he arrived at the B.B.C. after being boxing reporter for the *Daily Mail*.

Jimmy Connors was soon to forgive and forget. We had an amiable conversation in front of the camera at the next time of asking. Not so the *Radio Times*, which led its letters page with a strong complaint from Maidstone. 'My feeling,' wrote a Mrs Watts, 'is one of embarrassment. What will the Americans think of the British after the pompous way Peter West carried on? Who does he think he is? Connors is not a naughty child, to be chastised by an elder, but an intelligent sportsman . . . If Peter West's attitude typifies that of his friends in the Wimbledon hierarchy then I am surprised anyone bothers to enter the championships at all . . . I suggest that he sticks to "Come Dancing".'

Radio Times had the grace to invite my published reply to

this stricture, so I was able in respect of her advice about 'Come Dancing' to give the lady correspondent nought out of ten for originality. But there was no reflection in its pages of the widespread disgust felt by the sporting fraternity at the attitude of Connors to an historic occasion. So much for editorial balance – in the B.B.C.'s own journal.

In 1983, when the Wimbledon championships clashed with cricket's World Cup, Jonathan Martin as head of B.B.C. TV sport ordained that I should remain at the cricket. In 1984 he decided that I should continue to concentrate on that role. So my Wimbledon days were finished after twenty-seven summers.

It would have been nice to receive a note from someone at the B.B.C. to mark their end, but the old traditional courtesies seem honoured these days more in the breach than the observance. These mild reflections on declining social standards cannot mar overall the satisfaction derived from being part of a TV operation which set and maintained the highest standards in other respects. The B.B.C.'s style of tennis coverage has been copied throughout the world, even in the United States where they consider they have embellished their end-product by a restless direction of cameras and – to our way of thinking – a stream of blather from the commentary box. Those who suppose that British commentators talk their heads off should suffer a TV tennis course across the Atlantic, after which they might be grateful for the smallest mercies.

I have seen many great tennis encounters and great champions. One of the most memorable matches was that between Frank Sedgman and Pancho Gonzalez, in the days of the old professional circus, at Wembley Arena in 1956 – a gripping five-set affair when Dan Maskell and I shared the commentary and B.B.C. Television's then only channel unprecedently kept going until 1 o'clock in the morning. Those were the days when great professional players such as Lew Hoad and Ken Rosewall, hitching their circus across

the world and appearing for what their modern counterparts would regard as peanuts, accepted bad or dubious
decisions without demur and simply got on with the job. I
am not suggesting that the reactions of Pancho Gonzalez to
all situations were always phlegmatic. I recall his Wimbledon marathon, a marvellous first round match against
Charlie Pasarell in 1969, which lasted for a record five hours
and twelve minutes after being interrupted for bad light in
the evening's Stygian gloom. Gonzalez, from two sets down
and saving seven match points, eventually won through
22-24, 1-6, 16-14, 6-3, 11-9. No tie-break then.

That was the match after which the loser was asked
whether his father had been there to see it. 'Yeah,' Pasarell
replied. 'Did you look for the guy smoking two cigarettes at
once?' No one will suggest that Gonzalez was short on
charisma or style. I can see him now, flicking his sodden
shirt at the shoulder, crossing swords with the umpire in an
atmosphere which seemed supercharged. But I never saw
him bring tennis into disrepute. The game then was bigger
than any player.

Another Wimbledon contest etched firmly in my memory
is the semi-final of 1977 in which Bjorn Borg defeated his
friend, Vitas Gerulaitis, in five enthralling sets of the very
highest quality. There was scarcely an unforced error: every
single point, it seemed, had to be truly earned. Some of the
rallies were breathtaking in the conception and execution of
both players. In the other semi-final that year, a brash
young qualifier who had established a record by advancing
so far in the competition was put in his place by an elder
statesman. John McEnroe bowed out, with no obvious
charm, to Jimmy Connors in four sets.

Of all the men's singles finals I saw played at Wimbledon
the one between Stan Smith and Ilie Nastase in 1972, and
another, with Bjorn Borg and John McEnroe in 1980, are
those I remember as being the most riveting encounters. In
1972 outstanding players such as Rod Laver, Ken Rosewall,
Arthur Ashe and John Newcombe, who had won the title in

the two previous summers, were obliged to miss the championships because of their contracts with World Professional Tennis. But none of this seemed to matter much when Smith and Nastase locked horns on the Centre Court on a Sunday afternoon. It was the first time Wimbledon had staged its climax on the thirteenth day of the championships (the scheduled Saturday performance had been washed away by the rains). Smith and Nastase did the Sabbath, and a host of television viewers, proud. A Sunday men's final soon became the norm. Smith's victory, by 7-5 in the final set, owed as much to his temperament and resolution as to the remorseless pounding of his big and powerful game. Such qualities doubtless stood him in even better stead when, later that year, in front of the Romanian's own frenetic crowd in Bucharest, he beat the volatile Nastase again, this time in straight sets, in a crucial rubber in the Davis Cup challenge round. Moreover, a player whose game was geared to grass achieved that remarkable victory on a clay surface.

I have always admired Stan Smith, who epitomized the old-fashioned virtues of sportsmanship and perfect comportment on court in an era when young players were tempted to model themselves on the antics of a few elders. At that time no one produced more antics than Nastase. Here was an acknowledged genius when Jekyll's lyre gave out its richest tones but a different customer altogether when Hyde's gamesmanship (for which his opponents had another word) and his goading of officialdom took over. If Wimbledon had banned Nastase, as it could clearly have done within the rules obtaining years ago, the example might just have stopped the rot.

Back to a happier theme, to that tremendous final of 1980 in which Borg beat McEnroe 8-6 in the final set and so annexed his fifth successive Wimbledon title before at last, twelve months later, surrendering it to the same opponent. Towards the end of the last century William Renshaw won the Wimbledon crown six times in a row. Laurie Doherty did so five times in the early years of this one. But those players had only to play one final challenge round in order to preserve their status. Borg's record is approached in serious terms only by that of the Australian left-hander, Rod Laver, who won the title twice as an amateur, in 1961 and 1962, before he turned professional, and then twice more, in 1968 and 1969. That was after tennis, thanks to the initiative of Herman David and the All England Club, had gone 'open'.

Epic is one of those words that journalists tend to over-use but I think it fairly describes the final of 1980 which ended with most of us reflecting how sad it was there had to be a loser. It will be remembered mostly no doubt for the astonishing tie-break which enabled McEnroe to square the match with Bjorn Borg at two sets all. Put at its baldest, the tie-break lasted for twenty minutes and went finally to McEnroe 18-16. In its dramatic course Borg had five match points to add to a brace of them achieved in set number three, and McEnroe had seven points for the set. It was difficult to decide whose skills, daring or sheer guts one admired the more. Let no one suggest that tennis at this level does not require of its protagonists the most extreme mental and physical stamina. On that occasion it was Borg who held on for victory against an opponent never beaten until the last shot was played.

On the women's front it makes for pleasant reflection to recall three British successes: Angela Mortimer (whose husband is John Barrett) in the final against Christine Janes in 1961; Ann Jones against Billie-Jean King in 1969 after being there or thereabouts for years, and Virginia Wade, appropriately enough in the centenary summer of 1977, against Betty Stove (having first unlocked the door with a resounding semi-final victory over the defending champion, Chris Evert). Christine Truman, bless her, is these days in the B.B.C.'s radio team, remaining as natural, charming and unaffected as she was in her tennis heyday: she talks down-to-earth, practical sense. The team do a compelling job with

131

their amalgam of live and recorded commentary, reports and interviews. Those interviews for many years were conducted by Gerald Williams whose close relationship with the players, allied to a natural flair for the job and a professional journalist's antennae, produced some sparkling stuff. These days he has accepted a different challenge in television. I have done only one radio tennis commentary in my life; it was donkey's years ago during the old covered court championships at Queen's Club. I found it taxing to keep up with the speed of a men's doubles and admired the facile skills of Max Robertson, whose words per minute put a champion shorthand/typist in the shade. Over many years Max has been as much an annual part of Wimbledon on radio as Dan Maskell on the gogglebox.

But I digress from Wimbledon's distaff side. The best women's final I saw there was the one that matched Margaret Court against Billie-Jean King in 1970; two great champions and competitors, two players with a big, always aggressive game. On that occasion, they brought a match between women to heights which may not have been so long sustained before or since. The audience was held enraptured for all but two and a half hours. The Australian won a classic of its kind 14-12, 11-9; a total of forty-six games and still a record for the Wimbledon women's final. This was the third and last singles title won there by Margaret Court. It was Billie-Jean's fifth successive appearance in the last round. Billie-Jean has won more Wimbledon titles than anyone, man or woman. But Margaret's record number of big championships, which Martina Navratilova has so hungrily pursued, still stands. How would these two fare against each other, both of them at their peak? In physique and approach they have much in common. By a shade of odds it is likely that Martina's left-handed serve could make just the crucial difference.

I cannot write from first-hand knowledge of the legendary players of an earlier era. But I had the pleasure of interviewing Henri Cochet, Rene Lacoste, Jean Borotra and Jacques

Brugnon at Wimbledon's centenary championships. The recording of that conversation with the four musketeers of tennis was subsequently 'wiped' by some moron unmindful of tennis history. Mon dieu, quel ignorance! Of the men's champions I long thought that Rod Laver was the best I ever saw. Lew Hoad was magnificent on his day; I shall never forget the way in which he annihilated Ashley Cooper to win a second successive title before becoming a professional. Bjorn Borg's perhaps unassailable record speaks for itself. But having seen the heights which John McEnroe's game attained when he defeated Jimmy Connors in the final of 1984, I believe now that this American has been the greatest of them all.

Left handers both, Laver and McEnroe share the complete armoury: a big, swinging, varied serve (though McEnroe's is the more lethal on its day), touch, timing, flair, athleticism, and all the shots. But I think McEnroe, the direction of his passing shots on a two-fisted back-hand a little more disguised, may just have the edge with his superb racket handling and the flexibility which enables him to stay in a rally when under the most insistent pressure and sometimes to find a winning opening where none seems to exist.

I can add no original thinking to the chorus of revulsion felt for McEnroe's frequently appalling behaviour on court, although I would like to stress that until he turned his back on British tennis (apart from Wimbledon) he was a long and loyal supporter of the Benson and Hedges Championships at Wembley. It should also be said in his favour that he has never, to my knowledge, sought to cheat an opponent out of a point fairly earned. It so happens that when he argues about a line decision, more often than not he is likely to be in the right. Yet none of these things can be the slightest excuse for the loutish, street-urchin manner in which he has consistently lampooned officials. I have always thought his father must have a lot to answer for in what appears to have been a lamentable failure to discipline his offspring in the formative years. So have those whose duty it has been to frame the rules of the game. It should have been decreed years ago that any player insulting officials on court would be subject to instant suspension.

One final thought on the tennis front. Is it not grotesque that when in many places the grass roots of the game are crying out for support, a multi-millionaire such as Ivan Lendl can be rewarded – in addition to his king's ransom in prize money – with a gold and diamond-encrusted racket worth almost £500,000 for winning the European Champions' Championship three times in five years?

Back in the fifties a TV professional with claims to being regarded as an all-rounder might be expected to turn his hand to anything. This explains how I have come at one time or another to work on thirty-three different sports or pastimes: angling, archery, athletics, basketball, billiards, bowling, canoeing, clay pigeon shooting, cricket, darts, fencing, gliding, golf, gymnastics, hockey, ice hockey, judo, lacrosse, pentathlon, rowing, rugby union, small bore shooting, show jumping, snooker, squash, swimming, table tennis, tenpin bowling, tug-of-war, volleyball, water-skiing, weight-lifting and yachting.

In my younger days I read all the best books I could find about cricket and rugby, athletics and golf. In these sports I reckoned to know the history of great events and great performers. Yet for someone who became bound up with cricket in the summer, televised athletics and golf had to be strictly rationed. At least I had the pleasure of sharing commentary (with the late Norris McWhirter) on a memorable 5,000 metres race at the White City in 1954 when Christopher Chataway beat Vladimir Kutz, and of interviewing Arnold Palmer after he had won the Open golf title at Birkdale.

The Olympic Games of 1948, in London, presented my first opportunity to commentate on hockey. At a preliminary meeting of commentators at Broadcasting House the question was asked, 'Does anyone know anything about hockey?' I was the only one to put my hand up. Some years afterwards B.B.C. Television began its annual coverage of the women's international hockey match at Wembley. I was asked by my then cricket producer, Antony Craxton, to share the commentary with Marjorie Pollard, who had been an outstanding hockey and cricket player in her youth. We shared an agreeable chore for a dozen years and more, and I soon got wise to the idea of putting cotton wool in my ears as insulation against the cacophony of screaming schoolgirls enjoying a high old day out.

In 1960 I went to Rome to work at the first of five successive Olympic Games for television. I was pleased to be asked to cover the hockey tournament, this being the only one of five designated sports which I thought I could talk about without taking a crash course in the essentials. When it came to the final, alas, the B.B.C. were unsuccessful in a draw for the few available commentary positions at the venue itself. So when India came to play Pakistan in the last round I had the taxing job of doing a live commentary off the tube, while sitting next to David Coleman in the athletics stadium. This assignment, our Italian TV hosts assured us, would be made easier by the provision of a 'guide commentary' fed into our ears by an English-speaking observer at the actual scene. But this observer knew as little about hockey as the Italian TV producer whose cameras focused so close on the action that when the ball was hit out of one camera shot – and a hockey ball can travel a long way fast – I had little idea where it had gone to until another camera picked up its progress. Praise be, I got the goal scorers accurately identified and, after returning home, was never asked whether I had been at the match. At the end of it I remember saying, 'And now from the hockey over to David Coleman in the athletics stadium,' whereupon I gave him the microphone with one hand and a well known digital sign with the other.

I covered five Olympic rowing regattas, at two of them being condemned to talk about the finals when sitting in front of a monitor screen many miles distant. Commentators stationed at the end of a 2,000 metres course are grateful to the cameras for revealing how things are going for most of the race, but it becomes frustrating when a British boat struggles and the cameras concentrate on the leaders. How to sound adequately patriotic, or even well-informed, without an occasional close-up picture of the British entry?

When bound one day for the rowing course at the Tokyo Olympics of 1964 I found the traffic congestion even worse than usual and it soon became apparent that short of some very positive measures I would be late for a broadcast for only the second time in my career. The outside lane was, however, being kept open for the Crown Prince of Japan, son of the Emperor.

My Japanese driver, a student, spoke good English, 'When his Highness comes past,' I told him, 'get into the same lane and stick close to his tail.' The Japanese are not encouraged to show this sort of initiative and I think the driver had visions of committing hara-kiri. But to his eternal credit he did what I asked. We had a clear run for the last six miles, lights flashing, klaxons blowing and Japanese motor-cyclists following behind the royal personage affecting not to notice the strange vehicle tucked in behind them.

Four years later, in Mexico City, I was in the athletics stadium when the American, Ralph Beman, became the first man to leap through the 28-foot barrier in the long jump event. But, alas, just as he did so, my attention was distracted by a commotion in the crowd behind me, and my first sight of history being made was on television later that evening.

At the Munich Olympic Games of 1972, magnificently staged by West Germany but clouded by the appalling terrorist attack on the Israeli athletes, I thought to have some time to myself when returning late one evening from a stint at the rowing. Alan Hart, the editor in charge of our TV operation, had other ideas. 'We've just won two medals at the judo,' the chef d'equipe announced. 'There's no one else available, so I'd like you to do a live dub in half an hour.' My reaction was predictable. 'Don't worry,' he added. 'I've got John Goodbody to talk you through it.'

John Goodbody of the old London *Evening News* was a judo expert well able to prime a commentator who knew little about his sport. Without him I would have died a thousand deaths. As it was, the two of us had time for a quick look at the edited material before zero hour. Arriving home after the Olympics I was congratulated by several friends on my apparent mastery of a new sport. Blessings bountiful on John Goodbody and all the other experts – Benny Foster on cycling to name just one – who have enabled me when covering unfamiliar pursuits to sound as if I knew what I was talking about.

It was at Munich, I have to report, that I perpetrated a little gaffe at the rowing which is still recalled by my friends with some delight. In the women's pairs event the lady doing the steering for some of the crews was installed at the bow end of the boat. 'You'll notice the difference here,' I advised the viewers. 'The women carry their cox behind them.'

I was listed in the television team for Moscow in 1980 but was then left out of it when the United States withdrew their entry and the B.B.C. decided to cover the games with reduced numbers. I was thankful for that, having no particular desire to visit the Soviet Union. However, B.B.C. Television seems to hold firm to its belief that professionals, even ageing ones, are better value than subject experts when coping with certain sports under conditions of intense pressure. It was flattering to be asked to join their team yet again, in Los Angeles in 1984. By then I was four years older in the tooth, and asked to be excused. For the versatile Barry Davies there was a joy denied to me at all the Olympics I covered: he brought news of a medal for the British hockey team.

That mention of pressure reminds me of some hairy moments which were, I think, the worst I ever experienced in front of a camera. Many years ago I was summoned by the producer, Slim Wilkinson, to link, from London, the European championships staged in Yugoslavia. There came a point when everyone at the receiving end was getting pictures without the sound of commentary from David Coleman and Ron Pickering, who continued in blithe ignorance to do their stuff. An evident crisis at home base. 'You take up the commentary,' Slim yelled into my ear. 'We'll keep the picture going.'

No time or cause for argument, but I got no joy at all from seeking to identify the runners, almost all of whom I had never seen or heard of, in a heat of the 5000 metres. A hopeless business. I think Slim – and the viewers – stood the strain for several minutes while my all too obvious inadequacies were revealed. It seemed like an eternity to me. Eventually, thank the good Lord, Slim took mercy on everyone and, as the technical jargon has it, 'faded to black'.

'I wouldn't have wished that on my worst enemy,' the amiable Slim confessed afterwards. 'I think you've earned a gin and tonic.' I agreed with him, insisting on a double. The press critics, understandably enjoying the sight of P. W. and the B.B.C. making a mess of things, could not be blamed for making the most of it.

Chapter Seven

WHEN I WAS AT prep school, a Kentish shrine at which I worshipped was the old Angel cricket ground in Tonbridge. For an impressionable lad completing his scorecard with inky fingers there could never be too many instances of 'st Ames b Freeman' or too many runs from the peerless Frank Woolley, then approaching the end of his career. Little did I think that, many years on, I should have the joy of interviewing Woolley on television or of commentating on a match in which Les Ames, my greatest hero, played.

I never saw Frank Woolley bowl, so I cannot speak of all the versatile talents which made him in his prime one of the game's greatest all-rounders. But I retain memories of him pocketing catches at slip with practised comfort and of playing innings the like of which I have not seen mirrored since. His long reach, range of easeful shots and apparent disdain for the opposition enabled him to put bowling to the sword with unique elegance and power. He stroked rather than hit his runs, and I have always liked the story, apocryphal perhaps, of an occasion in a county game at Old Trafford when Dick Pollard's first ball in the Kent innings was dispatched over the sightscreen for six. 'I'm sorry, Dick,' Woolley said, 'I was pushing for a single.' Of all the left-handers I have seen, only the great South African batsman, Graeme Pollock, another tall man, has played quite like Woolley did.

Some of my last memories of first class cricket before the

war spanned a week and more in August 1938 beginning with the match at Canterbury between Kent and Australia. This had its disappointments for me, not least the running out of Frank Woolley off the first ball in the county's first innings. The great man made eighty-one second time around, and Les Ames got a rousing hundred, so my morale was restored. I also saw Bradman make a mere sixty-seven. I was sad that Stan McCabe and 'Tiger' O'Reilly were rested by the touring side. I never saw either of those famous Australians in action, but at least I can tell a tale about the Tiger. O'Reilly lost patience one day with the umpire, Bill Reeves, who had turned down his frequent appeals for lbw. He finally trapped a batsman – as he thought – in front of all three stumps and, wheeling round with an impassioned snarl, enquired: 'Well, how was *that* one, ump?' 'Ump?' Reeves said. 'You've been giving me the bloody ump all day. Not out.'

By all accounts Bill Reeves, whom I never met, was the ripest of characters. Another umpire in the same mould was the Leicestershire bowler, Alec Skelding. This dear old character was standing one day in a Somerset game at Bramall Lane when Colin McCool, the Australian Test cricketer, was hit full pitch on the pads. Skelding gave him out. 'I didn't even see the ball,' McCool confided as he passed the umpire on his way back to the pavilion. 'Neither did I,' Skelding said, 'but it's better to please 5,000 Yorkshiremen than one bloody Australian.'

Was it Skelding or Reeves who, when asked, 'How's that?' after a tearaway fast bowler had hit the batsman a fearful crack on his toecap, replied, 'Bloody painful, I should think. Not out.' Most cricketers will have heard that one. So also the tale about an aggrieved batsman, dismissed lbw, who on passing the umpire let it be known that he could not have been out in a month of Sundays. 'You don't think so?' the umpire rejoined. 'Then I suggest you look in the paper tomorrow morning.' But have you heard what the batsman said then? '*Me* look?' he enquired. 'I'm the editor.'

My last distant memory of O'Reilly is linked with a holiday beach in Devon and the resonant tones of Howard
Marshall describing on radio the frustrations of an Australian attack at the Oval when Len Hutton made his then
record Test match score of 364. Nobody, I suspect, was more
frustrated than Fleetwood-Smith, whose figures when
Hammond declared at 903 for 7 were 87-11-298-1. That was
the match in which Yorkshire's Arthur Wood, keeping
wicket for England instead of an injured Les Ames, was
seventh out for 53 with the total 876. Returning to the
dressing room he is reported to have flung his bat down and
declared, in mock despair, 'Just like me, getting out in a
bloody crisis.'

If I were asked to nominate the half-dozen or so cricketers
whose play has given me most pleasure I would put Denis
Compton, Keith Miller, Gary Sobers and Ian Botham at the
top of my list and then have the very dickens of a job to
decide about the others. I wrote a piece about Denis Compton in the *Daily Telegraph*, in celebration of his sixty-sixth
birthday in 1984, and I echo it here to salute the genius of a
cricketer the like of whom this and future generations will
be very fortunate to see.

My mind goes back to the golden summer of 1947 when
the names of an illustrious Middlesex duo, Compton and
Edrich, seemed forever linked in the headlines. Between
them, in all matches against the touring South Africans,
they plundered more than 2,000 runs. With eighteen hundreds and a season's aggregate of 3,816 Compton set records
that will never be surpassed so long as cricket's present first-
class structure remains. The records, stunning though they
were, and the bare statistics meant very little to an ever-
modest, dashing cavalier who tailored every innings to his
side's needs and never played a selfish one. There was an
eternal freshness, a gaiety, a sense of fun, enjoyment and
challenge about his batting that gave him box office appeal
and made him a folk hero of his time. An entertainer
supreme, and always an impeccable sportsman.

To his marvellous eye (the priceless gift of 'seeing the ball early') were added instinctive timing, balance, flexible wrists, nimble footwork, a complete armoury of strokes and a rare capacity for audacious improvization. If he had specialities, these were the sweep which got him out sometimes when the bounce was uneven but brought him countless runs (no one has played this shot more effectively), the cover drive and a delectable late cut. There have been more powerful and elegant cover drivers, but no one reduced cover points to such distraction as he opened or closed the blade to frustrate their latest move.

In other respects Denis Charles Scott Compton, CBE, was less well organised. In spite of his stout assertion, with a glint in eye, that he seldom ran anyone out, it has to be said that he was not the greatest judge of a run, and he cannot deny that he achieved the rare distinction of running out his brother in Leslie Compton's benefit match. John Warr (Cambridge University, Middlesex and England) has always maintained that Denis was the only batsman to call his partner for a single and wish him luck at the same time. His former county captain also holds that conversational par for the course was: 'Yes . . . no . . . wait . . . sorry . . . oh my gawd!'

If Denis arrived on time for a day's cricket – something that could never be taken for granted – it was always possible that he turned up without some vital piece of clothing or impedimenta. How many of his hundreds, I wonder, were made with borrowed bats? I am told that he made one of them, against India, without his socks on. He suffered lapses of concentration in the field where in his athletic prime he was an outstanding all-round performer. It was always said that he could catch anything, provided he happened to be looking. Another endearing weakness was his inability to say 'No' to any worthwhile request which explains how, as I have mentioned elsewhere, after his career was done he could find himself booked to play in three different matches on the same day.

How many first-class runs, how many hundreds (in addition to the 123 he finished with) would he have made but for years lost to the war and a creaking knee? The legacy of an old football injury in Arsenal's colours, it reduced his mobility in the later years of his career and finally impelled him to retire prematurely. That injury played no part in his slightly ungainly, rolling gait. E. W. Swanton has shrewdly observed that it was as though, when the construction of this creditable machine was completed, no one thought to go round and give the nuts and bolts a final turn.

The batting of Leonard Hutton, Compton's great England contemporary, was less exciting and unpredictable, although when he put his mind to it he could come up with an innings of breathtaking brilliance. A supreme technician, blessed with inexhaustible patience and concentration, he played the percentages like a mathematical guru knowing all the angles and possibilities. His skills against the finest bowling on a turning pitch made absorbing viewing. I could never be bored, even in his most defensive, intransigent moods, watching a master of his craft.

I could not say the same of another Yorkshireman whose equally professional, totally dedicated approach has never been in doubt. Nor can there be argument about the size and scope of Geoffrey Boycott's achievements. But if there is an element of selfishness in the play of almost all the great batsmen, let me just say that he has made it apparent a good deal more often than most. If one essential definition of a great batsman is that his play should be seen to be touched by genius, then Boycott, in spite of a monumental record, cannot be bracketed with Hutton and others. Another should be that great batsmen win matches rather than save them.

In the immediate post-war era, when English bowling was tenuous but English batting distinguished, Cyril Washbrook brought me joy with his belligerent reaction to short-pitched fast bowling. There was never a bonnier fighter than Bill Edrich; it may have been forgotten now that when he and Denis Compton took the game by storm in

1947, he was the first to reach 3,000 runs. Edrich relished a challenge and played his cricket like he has lived his life – to the full. When John Warr was invited to William's fourth wedding, an usher at the church, allocating seats for the guests, enquired of him, 'Bride or groom?' 'Don't worry,' John replied. 'I've got a season ticket.'

Those were the days when Walter Robins, upon winning the toss for Middlesex, would demand a total of 400 by 6 p.m. so that, if it suited his book, his bowlers might take a brief crack at the opposition before stumps were drawn. One of his opening batsmen was Jack Robertson, a cultured stylist and beau ideal for aspiring young right handers. That Robertson made a hundred at Lord's in a Test match in 1949, yet never played for England in this country again, testified to the strength of our batting in those days. His style has echoes in the play of Sunil Gavaskar, the most prolific run-maker and scorer of hundreds in Test match history: bat and pad together with never a shaft of daylight in between, no apparent weakness whatsoever and all textbook stuff. It is worth noting that Gavaskar has taken thirteen centuries off the formidable West Indian bowling – more than any other batsman.

In 1949 Walter Hadlee captained a New Zealand touring side with a batting strength so formidable that in one of our best summers it was always on the cards that the four Test matches, each played over only three days, would all be drawn. Bert Sutcliffe and Martin Donnelly, left handers both, were the particular stars and I put both of them, without a moment's hesitation, in my list of batsmen who have given me much delight. In his time at Oxford, where he was stand-off half in the rugby XV, Donnelly had the distinction of winning an England cap in the centre. In 1947, his 162 not out for the Gentlemen against the Players, which he made in three hours, was one of the finest innings I have seen; he reduced some good bowlers to the status of selling platers. He was a player of perfect balance, light on his feet, and his forte was the 'whipped' shot, wide of mid-on, which he seemed able to play to perfection almost regardless of the ball's length.

In 1950, English spectators had their first sight of the West Indian triumvirate of Weekes, Worrell and Walcott. The three Ws, all then in their prime, simply took English cricket by storm. Weekes and Walcott each made seven hundreds; Worrell contented himself with six, including a velvety innings of 261 against England at Trent Bridge and another double century, 241 not out, at Leicester. But Everton de Courcy Weekes on five occasions got 200 or more. In May, at the Oval, I saw him take 232 off a Surrey attack which included Alec Bedser and Jim Laker. In one passage of arms against the bowling of Surrey's captain, Stuart Surridge, who had just previously signed up Weekes to sponsor Surridge bats, the first four deliveries with the second new ball were all clattered for four. 'Steady on, Everton,' said Jack Parker, standing at slip. 'You'll be losing the contract.'

In the West Indians' next match, at Fenner's, Cambridge University declared at the respectable total of 594 for five, John Dewes (223) and David Sheppard (227) having shared an opening partnership of 343. Weekes then contributed 304 not out (in 325 minutes) and Worrell 160 to a West Indian innings of 730 for three. End of match. It was certainly a different game in those days. Weekes was nearing 300 when John Warr sent down what the bowler describes as the one he reserved only for the greatest of batsman. 'Look at all these people moving in front of the sightscreen,' Everton said to Frank. 'Come three.' This observation had a later echo at Bacup in the Lancashire League where Everton was joined one day by the youngest member of the side coming in at No. 11. 'When I hit the last ball of the over,' he said, 'you run to this end 'cos I'll be at that one.'

In June 1950, after the Nottinghamshire captain, Bill Sime, had been imprudent enough to put the West Indians in to bat, I witnessed Everton Weekes plunder 279, on a bland pitch, in five minutes under four hours. In this murderous innings, during the course of which he never took his sweater off, he hit 43 4s. But no sixes: putting the ball in the air he regarded as a needless risk. Returning to the pavilion enclosure, he was asked by a venerable county member why he had not gone on to beat C. G. Macartney's record of 345 in a day on the same ground, for the Australians, in 1921. 'Man,' Everton replied, 'nobody told me.'

After that he made 246 not out against Hampshire and 200 not out against Leicestershire, that last innings including the fastest hundred of the season, in 65 minutes, and a partnership of 309 with Worrell in less than two and a half hours. Weekes, no doubt about it, was a killer. I watched most of the West Indians' matches on that tour and I rate him the best of a famous triumvirate. Worrell was the most cultured and elegant, Walcott the fiercest hitter, notably off the back foot. But Weekes with his range of shot and appetite for runs was devastating.

Jim Laker asked him one day why he had been christened Everton. 'My Dad,' the reply came, 'was a soccer nut and a mad keen supporter of Everton.' 'A good job,' observed Jim, 'that he wasn't a fan of West Bromwich Albion.'

Containing the three Ws in 1950 posed problems such as those faced on one occasion by a young amateur Leicestershire captain who was not highly regarded by his older players. At his wits' end half an hour before the close after the opposition had raised 400 for one wicket, he took counsel with his senior professional, George Geary. 'Who shall I put on now, George?' he enquired. 'If I were you,' George replied, 'I should put the bloody clock on and we can all go home.'

Two summers before Weekes and company first came to England we had seen a young prodigy who, when his Test career was finished sixteen years later, then stood second only to Bradman in the Australian lists for runs and hundreds scored, and for the size of his average. Neil Harvey, only five foot six inches tall, was a swarthy left hander of exceptionally exciting gifts. He had all the shots together with scintillating footwork and a challenging attitude to bowlers which ensured that he could never be dull. Richie Benaud has written that in Australian cricket Harvey was the most difficult batsman he ever bowled at. Harvey was also a magnificent all-round fielder, as good as any I have seen.

I wonder what figures Peter May might have finished with had his career not come to a premature conclusion through illness and, I suspect, some disenchantment with the pressures exerted by the media on a man who had captained his country more often than any other. In discounting Len Hutton and Denis Compton, whose careers began in the thirties, I rate May as the best England batsman to have emerged since the war. Of all right handers in any era I can recall, he was the finest on-side player. But he had a complete armoury of strokes and a temperament burnished with steel. He played the game hard, yet never to anything but the highest standards of sportsmanship.

Colin Cowdrey under full sail made batting look the simplest occupation in the world. He leant into his strokes with glorious timing and unhurried ease. His bat seemed that much broader than others'. Yet there were occasions when he seemed to doubt his own enormous capacity; a great player of enigmatic mood. I have seen slip fielders more athletic, more acrobatic, but none, I think, more secure and dependable when the catches came within a reasonable compass.

By the start of the 1986 season in England, no batsman still living had made more first-class runs (47,793) than Tom Graveney. Yet in assessing the qualities of Graveney as a batsman, mere figures – though amply confirming his status – seem far less important than the way in which he made his runs. Tall, upstanding, always fluent and graceful, he seemed incapable of playing a crude stroke. William Lillywhite, a great old Sussex bowler, wrote of Joseph Guy (Notts and All England) that he was 'elegance, all elegance, fit to play before the Queen in her parlour'. Graveney's batting, his play on the off-side a joy to behold, also conjured such thoughts. No right handed batsman has tickled my taste buds more.

147

Ted Dexter's batting made, in contrast, a thrilling assault on the senses. Not for nothing was he known as Lord Edward: he played like a peer of the realm, the bowlers on his great days made to represent the lower House. No one in the post-war era can have hit a cricket ball more cleanly and decisively in a fashion to delight the purists, though one or two, notably Clive Lloyd and Ian Botham, may have struck it a mite harder. I suspect there were several echoes in Dexter's play of A. C. Maclaren, by all accounts a batsman of imperious attitude who was said to dismiss a wretched bowler from his lordly presence. Of some breathtaking innings I saw Dexter play none was more memorable than the seventy he made against Wes Hall and Charlie Griffith at Lord's in 1963. How might England have fared against the latest West Indies side if they had had a Dexter to throw down the gauntlet to their pace attack?

While Dexter was still in his prime an outstanding batsman, Graeme Pollock, arrived on the South African scene and not long afterwards there came another, Barry Richards: two players fit to rank with the greatest of any era but denied by politics, for most of their careers, the Test match cricket which should have been their stage. I had seen enough of Pollock on South Africa's short tour of England in 1965 to bracket him alongside Frank Woolley, with whom in physique and power of easeful shot he had much in common. At Trent Bridge that summer, on a pitch declared by the pundits to be too slow for dashing stroke-play, he confounded the theorists with one of the finest hundreds I can recall. The last 91 of them, out of 102, were gathered in little over an hour. He was then twenty-one.

Richards was a superb technician in the classical mould, his play likewise touched by genius. In a brilliant double hundred I saw him make against Nottinghamshire at Portsmouth he danced down the pitch to the faster bowlers, toying with an attack in the way that Denis Compton used to do.

An Australian of much the same era was Greg Chappell,

who finished his long and distinguished Test career with more runs for his country than anyone else, including Bradman, and all of them made with style. There can have been few right handers with such mastery of the ball pitched on their legs; his on-driving matched that of Peter May in assurance if not quite in severity. To his enviable talents as a batsman he added those of an outstandingly good slip fielder and a useful change bowler.

I have so far omitted Keith Miller from my list of favourite Australians, preferring to write of him as one of the great all-rounders. The same applies to Gary Sobers and Ian Botham. So I write briefly now of four more batsmen from overseas, three of them West Indians, who have enriched my days as a camp follower. Of these, Rohan Kanhai has been the most excitingly unpredictable, Clive Lloyd the most potent, Vivian Richards the most exceptionally gifted and Zahir Abbas of Pakistan the most cultured. Kanhai has destroyed attacks with a flashing rapier, Lloyd with a broadsword, 'Zed' with a delicate knife and Richards with a combination of all these weapons. If Richards has an Achilles heel, it is his reluctance, born of understandable arrogance, to play himself in, as others have to do. He can be careless. But why should I dwell on the trifling weakness of a cricketer who has reduced so many attacks to frustrated impotence and played innings the like of which no contemporary batsman could match?

My last batsman is David Gower. You could not imagine the England captain playing a crude or jarring shot, but that has not stopped him getting out too often in ways unworthy of his talents. When things are not going for him, the long hops and leg-side full tosses tend to find unwanted targets. He has been vulnerable to quick bowling slanted across him because his footwork has not always brought him into line. Yet after an unpromising start to the waterlogged season of 1985 he enjoyed a marvellous series against Australia. From a batsman whose sense of touch and timing is unsurpassed in the present era we may expect a flow of graceful runs for years to come.

The Australian side Gower put to his rapier in 1985 was admittedly a poor one. When setting off for the Caribbean last January he needed no reminding that it would be a totally different ball game out there, yet he still managed to total the best part of 400 Test runs and to average not far short of 40. Against a four-man pace attack of unrelenting ferocity, that was an achievement in itself. I leave the matter of his captaincy to my postscript, but I allude to it in general terms – I think charitably – on page 164.

It seemed that England's batsmen never quite came to a firm conclusion about how they should confront the bouncers. Should they have gone bravely for the hook shot – with inevitable risk of a top edge if the ball was too high or, when it was not, of physical injury if they failed to move across, *outside* the line of it? Should they have taken regular evading action (which is not so simple as it sounds when a 90 mph delivery is whistling up your windpipe). Some of the finest players of fast bowling in the past, when facing short-pitched stuff just as intimidating though much less frequent, evolved a safe if negative reaction by *never* taking their eyes off the ball. In this respect the name of Reggie Simpson (Notts and England) comes particularly to mind.

To have seen Jack Hobbs make a hundred, and Larwood and Voce bowl in harness, are joyful memories to take through my dotage. The sight of Larwood – before the 'bodyline' series in Australia in 1932–3 – was more than enough to convince a star-struck lad that no one could have bowled faster. Twenty years on, I believed that the 'typhoon', Frank Tyson, was quicker still – an opinion shared by both teams when he destroyed Australia's batting on Len Hutton's victorious tour in 1954–5. Two decades later the England batsmen on another visit to that country rated Jeff Thomson as an explosive, holy terror in pace. In the latest era Michael Holding must have been almost as fast, his fearsome pace disguised by a silken, athletic approach.

How can we ever say for sure which have been the

greatest fast bowlers, so many of them working in tandem? Consider the outstanding pairs of the post-war era – Lindwall and Miller, Trueman, Statham and Tyson (perming any two from three), the South Africans Adcock and Heine (rated by Denis Compton as the sharpest and nastiest of all), Davidson and McKenzie, Hall and Griffith, Lillee and Thomson, Roberts and Holding, Holding and Garner, Garner and Marshall, Willis and Botham. Add to this hall of fame the names of Sobers, Snow, Richard Hadlee, Kapil Dev and Imran Khan, and my list of candidates is complete. It includes five brilliant all-rounders whose versatile talents I reserve for another section.

The most versatile, most successful (and most talkative) English fast bowler of my time has been Frederick Sewards Trueman. Quarried in a Yorkshire coal mine, he is now one of the world's staunchest believers in a capitalist society and a government a long way to the right of centre. Of the England fast men who have taken more than 200 Test wickets, Trueman's striking rate has been the best: he collected his then record 307 victims at an average of 21.57, which is three or more runs better than that of any other. Of all the England bowlers with more than 150 Test wickets, only Sydney Barnes (by some way – 189 at 16.43) and Jim Laker (marginally – 193 at 21.24) have better averages.

Of the sundry stories about Trueman I am content here to mention two. The first of them concerns his second wedding. 'There has been disputation here today,' the groom observed at the reception afterwards, 'about who is fastest bowler in England. Some say Tyson is, some say Statham and some say Trueman. All I can tell you lot is that tomorrow morning I'll be bloody slowest.' The second features his characteristic reaction to a remark passed in the 'Test Match Special' radio enclave when television, during a break for rain, was putting out film of a series in which F. S. T. had starred. 'Fred,' somebody observed. 'You don't look as fast as some of the quicks today.' 'Of course I don't,' Fred riposted. 'It's in bloody black and white.'

John Woodcock remarked one day in *The Times* that Trueman had taken over 300 Test match wickets in his playing days and several thousands more on the radio since. Fred's fruity and sometimes dogmatic criticisms of modern cricket have not been consistently well received in the dressing rooms. But this great bowler and great character has never been diffident. I have always enjoyed working with him on those few occasions when he joined the TV team. Wind him up in an interview and you can then sit back for several minutes considering a further question. I have found Geoff Boycott to be equally accommodating at such times.

If Brian Statham was the straightest, most consistent and most dependable of England's fast bowlers in the post-war years, Bob Willis has surely been the most indomitable. In spite of injuries which would have spelled the end for a man of less determination, Willis managed to give his Test career several new leases of life. In an honest, uncomplicated fashion he hurled himself into the task, wheeling away with persistent accuracy, relying on bounce as well as movement off the pitch to sharpen his claws. It stands much to Willis's credit as a captain that he upheld old standards of behaviour on and off the field but, as I think John Woodcock sagely observed in *The Times*, he too often as leader switched on to auto-pilot. A fast bowler should not, as a general principle, be asked to captain a side; he has quite enough on his plate. Willis did his honest best with dignity.

I shall always think of Hall as the most spectacular and chivalrous of fast bowlers from the Caribbean, and of Charlie Griffith, his partner in arms, as the meanest in spirit. Big Charlie had a chip on his shoulder and sometimes a bent arm which made him perhaps the nastiest of them all to face. I rate Joel Garner as the meanest in a wholly different sense – arguably the most effective limited-over bowler of his era. But I am inclined to think that the most remarkable performance I saw by a West Indian fast bowler occurred against England at the Oval in 1976, when Michael Holding, purring in from the Vauxhall end, had 8 for 92 and 6 for 57, hitting the stumps no fewer than nine times *on a slow, unresponsive pitch*.

If I were asked to nominate my opening fast bowlers for a world team chosen from post-war players I would at once write down Ray Lindwall and then ask myself how I dare put his name in front of a man, Dennis Lillee, who has taken more Test wickets (355) than anyone else in the history of the game. Lillee, moreover, acquired them at an average of just over five a match, a rate exceeded only by the Englishman, Sydney Barnes. The two Australians had a great deal in common. Both ran up to the wicket with a smooth, accelerating approach. Both had a lovely action, though in Lindwall's case the arm perhaps was not quite so high as the stylists demanded. Both in their prime had extreme speed and hostility, and to these qualities as their careers unfolded were added control, and a mastery of swing and cut, the yorker and change of pace. Lindwall used the bouncer more sparingly (and never, so far as I remember, against tail-enders).

I saw Lindwall bowl a remarkable over in the match against Surrey at the Oval in 1953. A young P. B. H. May had by then established himself in the England side but now faced an Australian attack for the first time. I would swear now, all these years afterwards, that Lindwall in running through the gamut of a fast bowler's craft had May playing and missing at all six balls. Not so. A glance at *The Fight for the Ashes*, the first of two books I wrote about successive Australian tours here, reveals that May did well at the last instant to withdraw his bat from two opening outswingers. He padded up to an inswinger which all but hit off stump and was beaten all ends up by another, faster outswinger. Surviving this ordeal by fire, he was yorked by Ron Archer to finish the game with scores of 0 and 1. England picked May for the first Test, in which he made 9, and for the last match of the series in which he played two useful innings.

Walter Robins, an England leg-spinner and forthright captain of Middlesex, said to Sydney Barnes one day, 'You bowled against all the great batsmen of the Golden Age after the turn of the century. Who caused you the most problems?' Sydney gave the matter his brief consideration. 'That feller Victor Trumper bothered me a bit,' he replied. 'He used to hit me over my head.' Robins pressed him further. 'And who else gave you trouble?' he enquired. 'Oh,' Sydney said, 'I never had any trouble with anybody else.' No wonder he is remembered as 'the greatest bowler of them all.'

Barnes was still harvesting League wickets at minimal cost when approaching his sixties. This was about the time when I had my first sight of Maurice Tate, a great medium-fast bowler who was nearing the end of his career with Sussex. A big man of jovial appearance, with feet splayed wide, he moved swiftly in to the wicket off a short run and with a classic action sent down late-swerving outswingers which fizzed even faster off the pitch. Barnes's pace was, I believe, something about genuine medium. Tate's surely was faster – akin through the air to that of Alec Bedser who has no one to challenge him seriously for the title of the world's best medium-fast bowler since the war.

In Surrey's great championship years of the fifties Alec Bedser certainly was not short of support from his fellow bowlers Loader, Laker and Lock, but when he first played for England after the war he often operated without much help from the other end – and often, too, against some immensely powerful Australian batting.

In his early days Bedser was an inswing bowler of impeccable length and persistence. Then the discovery and honing of a leg-cutter made him, in helpful conditions, a yet more daunting proposition. For twenty-three years – thirteen of them as Chairman – Bedser served as a national selector, giving unstinting service to the game he loves and respects. The latest generation of cricketers tends to think that his needle gets stuck in the groove as he goes on about the old virtues of line and length, of playing straight, of dedicated practice. Perhaps it does, but it repeats some timeless truths.

Bedser and Trueman shared England's opening attack

against India on a green pitch at Old Trafford in 1952. Fred, with a gale at his back in the first innings, had 8 for 31, causing no little alarm in opposing ranks. At the start of India's second innings Bedser, ball gripped in a massive hand, ran back to his mark at the Stretford end. 'Never seen you in so much of a hurry,' someone observed. 'A poor bugger like me,' Alec rejoined, 'can't afford to waste time when he gets the wind.'

It may have been later in that series when Godfrey Evans, standing up behind the stumps to the great man's bowling, picked up a very difficult low catch. 'How about that?' enquired Godfrey, rightly pleased with himself. 'It was off the bottom edge.' 'Of course it was,' said Alec. 'I can't get the ball any higher on this sodding wicket.' Indian traumas against Trueman at Old Trafford produced one of the better misprints in a local newspaper. 'When Umrigar,' the report went, 'missed a despairing hit at Trueman his balls went flying, one landing thirty yards behind the wicket.'

'Our Jim was one of the most fox-headed bowlers that ever bowled, and was enough to worry and puzzle any man alive.' Thus did old William Lillywhite write in days long ago of a fellow professional whose seductive artistry we see mirrored far less often in a cricketing age when sheer fire power and too often the intimidation of fast bowling holds the key to success on covered pitches.

I was held in thrall, as batsmen were, by the sight of Jim Laker, arguably the greatest of all off-spinners, bowling all day. The West Indian, Lance Gibbs, who gave the ball a considerable tweak, may have been the best of his kind on a hard, bland pitch, but he did not much like bowling round the wicket and he did not have Laker's devastating capacity on helpful surfaces. Jim was a bowler for all seasons with every skill and trick of his trade. England's selectors still managed to leave him out when M.C.C. toured Australia in 1950–1 and 1954–5. When at last they chose him to go there, under Peter May in 1959, he took more wickets than anyone else and headed both the Test and first-class averages.

I have always had a soft spot for Tony Lock, the other half of a famous Surrey duo, if only because he is the only England bowler against whom I have made a hundred. I hasten to add that he was only sixteen at the time. Zestful, aggressive, always totally committed, Lock also destroyed batsmen on turning pitches – and enjoyed a second prosperous career, in different conditions, as captain of Western Australia in Perth, to which city he long ago emigrated. It remains a remarkable fact that when Laker made history at Old Trafford by taking 19 wickets against Australia in 1956, Lock got only one.

How fortunate England were in the fifties to have a great pair of Surrey spinners as well as the Yorkshireman, Johnny Wardle, whose versatility was such that he could operate in the classic slow left hander's style or bowl chinamen and googlies out of the back of the hand. It was largely with the latter method that Wardle took twenty-six Test wickets and a record ninety all told on England's tour of South Africa in 1956–7. On the tour of the West Indies in 1953–4 England played Laker, Lock *and* Wardle in two Tests, and won them both by nine wickets. Shades of Chandrasekhar, Bedi and Prasanna or Venkat for India in a later era.

Of all the slow bowlers I have seen none gave me greater joy than Bishen Bedi with his rhythmic approach, classic action, great patience and voluptuous flight – ever willing, as I imagine were Colin Blythe and Wilfred Rhodes in a different age, to buy his wickets. 'Chandra', who destroyed England at the Oval in 1971, bowled his leg and top spinners almost as briskly as Doug Wright did for Kent and England. Both on helpful pitches achieved a disconcerting degree of bounce. Wright also had a lethal googly. With his long, bounding run he was a bowler whose Test figures did scant justice to one who frequently beat the bat yet somehow missed everything else as well. He was always respected by his greatest opponents. A modest, genuinely humble man, he looks many years younger than his seventy-two. There must be something about Kentish air.

The same reflection might be made about Derek Underwood, now forty-one and still bringing to his daily task the high skills and dedication of a bowler unique in style. There was never a greater trier than Derek, and today's county cricketers have no better example of how a professional should approach his job both on and off the field. Les Ames regards him, and I'm not inclined to disagree, as the greatest 'killer' on a damp pitch he has seen. Les, on spring-heeled feet, delighted to go down the wicket to the slower men. 'I could never have done it against Derek,' he says. 'I'd have been dead if I tried.' There are not many damp surfaces for Derek these days, but he keeps wheeling away. I wonder how many Test wickets he would have taken had he not played for Kerry Packer.

I can't end my impressions of the slow men without brief reference to the great West Indian pair, Ramadhin and Valentine, who arrived in England in 1950 to take fifty-nine wickets between them in four Tests, and to play so crucial a part in their country's first victorious series in England. Few left handers can have had greater powers of spin than Valentine. No one, I suspect, has ever mesmerized English batting as effectively as Ramadhin managed to do, although Cyril Washbrook battled his way to a hundred at Lord's and Len Hutton hit a masterly not out double hundred at the Oval, where Denis Compton was able to play in his one Test that summer. The perplexing nature of Ramadhin's spin was not finally rumbled until Peter May and Colin Cowdrey made 411 together at Edgbaston in 1957 and, by playing for turn from leg, with front pad thrust well down the pitch, reduced a genius to frustration.

Neither of those remarkable spinners from the Caribbean had played much first-class cricket when 1950 dawned. There is a story that when the West Indians were introduced to King George VI at Lord's, His Majesty said to Ramadhin, 'I've heard a lot about you.' 'Yessir,' the little man is alleged to have replied. 'I've heard a lot about you too.'

*   *   *

Since at least the days of the First World War there has never been a decade such as the eighties for redoubtable all-round skills. Ian Botham, Richard Hadlee, Imran Khan and Kapil Dev (placed here purely in alphabetical order) comprise a quartet whose combined haul of Test wickets comfortably tops the 1,000 mark and whose aggregate of Test runs was well into five figures in 1985. I name only nine more players who must rank as the outstanding all-rounders of the post-war era. These are Keith Miller, Vinoo Mankad, Trevor Bailey, Richie Benaud, Alan Davidson, Gary Sobers, Tony Greig, Eddie Barlow and Mike Procter.

Keith Miller was one of that rare breed of cricketers whose talents and compulsive appeal left the barmen with few customers. As a fast bowler he could turn the tide in a Test match in a couple of overs. His batting, often thrilling in conception and execution, could never be mundane. He was a magnificent catcher at slip. He played life to the full both on and off the field, and was a dashing, always chivalrous opponent with a wide range of interests and a genuine concern for the affairs of other people.

A tally of 2,109 runs and 162 wickets in Test cricket gave Vinoo Mankad an overall record exceeded only amongst Indians by Kapil Dev, who has played far more often for his country. Mankad was a slow left arm bowler of tireless persistence and guile in the early post-war years. That was the era of Trevor Bailey, unarguably England's finest all-rounder of the modern era until the arrival of Tony Greig, who in almost all ways was as different from him as chalk from cheese. We remember Bailey so often taking root at the crease with infinite grit and resource, and Greig leading a cavalry charge. Bailey in 61 Tests had 2,290 runs and 132 wickets. Greig in three fewer had 3,599 (averaging 40) and 141. Greig was an inspirational captain, leading from the front, but with no obviously profound gifts as a tactician or setter of fields. Bailey was never invited to lend his astute mind to the England captaincy.

Although he never made a Test match hundred, Alan

Davidson must be in my list as an always dangerous lower-order batsman, a marvellous all-round fielder and a great left arm opening bowler who captured 186 wickets at an average of only 20. His powers of late swing I have seen equalled at the highest level by very few. Surrey's Peter Loader was one of them. Gary Sobers was another. It is interesting to reflect that Australia have not produced a world class all-rounder since the days of Davidson and Richie Benaud, who still stands second to Dennis Lillee in the all-time list of their wicket-takers, with 248, and is one of only five cricketers with more than 2,000 runs and 200 wickets to their name. He was also an electric close fielder.

With a total of 8,032 Test match runs, 235 wickets and 110 catches, the figures of Sir Garfield St Aubrun Sobers need no embellishment. As three bowlers in one, having begun his Test career as an orthodox slow left arm bowler, then turning his hand to chinamen and googlies and finishing as a fast swinger of the ball over the wicket, he has been the most versatile of them all. To all his wondrous gifts he added an unfailingly happy temperament, an impeccable sense of sportsmanship and a warm and generous spirit. He surely commands a place in everyone's eclectic side chosen from all the eras of the game. And surely, too, Ian Botham must now have staked his claim to a similar status.

How wrong the pundits were to believe, some seasons past, that the loss of an outswinger from his armoury would reduce Botham to being just another Test bowler. Even without that potent weapon he roared back in 1985, bowling against Australia with all his pristine fire and pace, to take more wickets for England than anyone else.

He has always been prepared to buy his wickets, and he has had a rare talent for persuading batsmen to knock long hops (or intended bouncers) straight down the throat of long-leg. But you need a great deal more than luck to become the greatest English wicket-taker in history. An immense slip field, some of his catches defy belief. As a batsman, I rate him as a Titan.

I cannot believe that Gilbert Jessop or any other batsman of the past struck the ball with such tremendous power. The sheer physical strength of a very powerful man, his eye, his sense of timing, the big pick-up of a heavy bat hitting straight through the line, all contribute to a thrilling end-product. When Botham goes in to bat the bars empty just as swiftly as they did in the heyday of Denis Compton, Keith Miller and Ted Dexter. But English cricket's most charismatic hero since Compton, though idolized by the young, has not consistently endeared himself to all their seniors.

His impulsive nature leads him to shoot from the hip, and he sometimes behaves in a boorish fashion. It is regrettable that someone put on a pedestal by young people should have been associated publicly with drugs. It was distasteful, and wholly contrary to the ethos of the game, when he dismissed a batsman with two-fingered signs – though I think he has tried conscientiously, following pressure from above, to banish this supposedly macho exhibition from his repertoire. The sight of him expectorating on the field is no more attractive than when those in tennis or football indulge the habit.

Yet he remains in essence a big-hearted, open-handed man, and we all doff a respectful cap to him for his prodigious walk, from John o'Groats to Land's End, on behalf of leukaemia research. I would not, as I write this, bet against him riding through the Alps on an elephant. But I do say that a very forceful character needs strong and sensible management, and only time will tell if the guidance he gets from his imaginative new guru, Tim Hudson, will be fruitful as well as rational. The idea of setting up a so-called 'All Stars' team to play here outside the present structure of the game is one for the birds, and will be stoutly – and rightly – resisted by the establishment. If Tim Hudson can turn Ian into a Hollywood star, the best of British luck to one and all.

This and my next paragraph, added at page-proof stage, must echo a belief that not all readers, certainly not those amongst the West Indian cricket public, will agree with all

160

Outside Broadcast from Ghent in 1961 reporting on *Le Grand Cirque de France*.

(*Above*) With Mike Hawthorn at Silverstone shortly before his death in a road accident.

(*Below*) This was one of the regular cricket sides, mostly composed of broadcaster and journalists, which Brian Johnston took to play John Pawle's XI in an annua fixture at Widford in Hertfordshire. Standing (left to right): Peter Lloyd, John Woodcock, myself, Michael Melford, John Warner (son of Sir Pelham), Arthu Wrigley. Seated: Antony Craxton, Lionel Marson, an apparently non-playing captain, E. W. Swanton, Max Robertson. In front: Graham Alston, Rex Alsto

n Mike Burton (standing) and John Pullin (captain) on England's rugby tour of
tralia in 1975. This shot was taken by John Reason, then the *Daily Telegraph*
espondent. These days his trenchant, always widely read columns appear in
Sunday Telegraph.

Talking to Geoffrey Boycott, hotfoot from the crease at Headingley in 1977, aft
he had become the first player in cricket history to make his hundredth hundr
in a Test match. All this against the old enemy, Australia, and in front of the
Yorkshire faithful. The hero of the hour, understandably enough, was not
reluctant to talk on television before climbing into his bath. *Ken Kelly*

(*above*) After the 1977 Headingley Test match, a conversation with Test captains
~~g~~reg Chappell and Mike Brearley, whose England side had just won back the
~~a~~shes with a third successive victory in the series. All this occurred shortly before
~~th~~e cricket world was rocked by the Kerry Packer affair. *Ken Kelly*

(*below*) Headingley again, but five years on – and a chat with Bob Willis and Imran
~~Kh~~an, captains respectively of England and Pakistan. It is rare in cricket history
~~for~~ both sides to be led by fast bowlers in a Test series. This one went 2-1 to
~~En~~gland after a win by three wickets in the last match. *Ken Kelly*

(*Above*) A 1981 photograph of some of the television cricket team. Standing (fro[m]
left): Ted Dexter, Richie Benaud, Michael Fordham (scorer), Peter Pickering (i[n]
charge of captions and computerized output). Sitting: Jim Laker, David Kenni[ng]
(producer), myself and Tom Graveney. Kenning and Fordham, alas, both die[d]
not long after this shot was taken, and Jim Laker sadly passed on just as a ne[w]
cricket season was due to start on 23 April 1986.

(*Below*) With a famous (and unrivalled) Kentish line of wicketkeepers. From t[he]
left: Alan Knott, W. H. V. 'Hopper' Levett, Leslie Ames and the irrepressibl[e]
Godfrey Evans. I got in on the act after we had all celebrated Les Ames's eightie[th]
birthday at the St Lawrence ground, Canterbury, in December 1985. *Kentish
Gazette courtesy of Arthur Palmer*

ore the England rugby XV beat New Zealand at Twickenham in 1983, I
aged, on behalf of the *Daily Telegraph*, to inspire a gathering in Cambridge of
f the men who in 1936 had shared in England's first and only other victory
 the All Blacks in this country. Standing with me (from left): Bill Weston
ker), Dr Edward Nicholson (hooker) and Hal Sever (wing). Seated:
or-Gen. Sir Douglas Kendrew (prop and pack leader), Bernard Gadney
um-half and captain) and Peter Cranmer (centre). *Daily Telegraph*

This is Hector, a handsome flat-coated black retriever who belongs to our son Simon and his wife Valerie.

my thoughts about Ian Botham. By almost every token his tour of the Caribbean earlier this year was a personal disaster. By his own dizzy standards on the field his all-round return from the Test series fell lamentably short of expectation. He has still to take a Test hundred off West Indies' bowling. It cannot be gainsaid that on two tours of the Caribbean his Test batting average is a miserable 12.05.

That he should have been hounded by tabloid news reporters (not by cricket writers) through his activities, real or imagined, off the field is a matter for sympathy tempered by the reflection that many of his wounds are self-inflicted. He and his fellow players are entitled to some privacy, but Botham is a man who has never found it easy to keep a low profile. How very different a cricketing hero's progress can be when he is king of his castle in the middle and his side is winning too. My fervent hope that by the time these words are read at the end of another summer he will have made the front pages only for the best of cricketing reasons cannot, alas, be fulfilled.

Tim Hudson might give thought to a similar career for Imran Khan and Kapil Dev, two handsome men with a big following on the distaff side. There is not much between them when it comes to their batting figures in Test matches but if Kapil might play a more devastating innings, Imran, with an average in the low twenties, has a distinct edge as a bowler. Both now have the 300 wickets mark within their sights, but New Zealand's greatest all-rounder passed that milestone early in 1985. Richard Hadlee is at thirty-five now a master of his craft. His short, economical run-up should help to keep him going for a while yet. By the start of 1986 he was the most rounded and versatile of all the fast men, and I rejoice that so nice a man as his father, Walter, should have been followed in the family by such an outstanding and respected scion.

In his 30 Test matches for South Africa the combatant Eddie Barlow made more than 2,500 runs and gathered 40 wickets. Mike Procter in only 7 had not then made a big impact as a batsman but took 41 wickets at the remarkable average of 15. What, I wonder, would their final records have been if they had been able to tread a constant Test match stage, and how many more runs might Procter have made for Gloucestershire if he had concentrated on his batting?

When my two boys went to indoor cricket school at Eltham in the early sixties, Kent were running their eye over a lad, Alan Knott, whose skills as an off-spinner were then thought to be almost as exciting as the quality of his wicket-keeping. Knott, I think, has been the most brilliantly consistent wicketkeeper of the post-war era, although in my book he gets the verdict only by the shortest of hairs over Godfrey Evans and Bob Taylor.

No one was more reliable than the self-effacing Taylor with his subtly polished skills. He took some remarkable catches, but his more acrobatic rivals were capable of taking catches that defied belief, and I am certain that Alec Bedser, for whom Evans always stood up to the stumps, will always rate that 'inspirational' keeper as being without a peer. If it be said of Evans that he needed the biggest occasions to bring out his brilliant best, I will only add that his best set standards that could not be bettered. I am not at all sure why almost all of the outstanding wicketkeepers have come from England and Australia, although Wasim Bari's sustained record for Pakistan demands an honourable mention, and the credentials of the Springbok, 'Jock' Cameron, as a wicketkeeper/batsman between the wars must not be overlooked.

From the Great War onwards, in a distinguished English line, there were Herbert Strudwick (whose Test career began in 1911), George Duckworth and Leslie Ames. Between the wars 'Bertie' Oldfield must win the Australian palm. In the modern era Australia have had Don Tallon, a stylist in the Oldfield mould, followed by more pragmatic yet immensely effective performers such as Gil Langley,

Wally Grout, and Rodney Marsh. Richie Benaud held the very highest opinion of Grout's qualities. The double-act of Marsh and Lillee has been one of the deadly combinations of Test match history.

I saw George Duckworth keep wicket when I was a lad and subsequently had the pleasure of working with him on B.B.C. Radio in the north. I remember giving an account of a particular incident and then hearing him tell listeners in his blunt and endearing fashion, 'What really happened was this.' I do not doubt that he was a more spectacular, certainly noisier, wicketkeeper than the hero of my schooldays, but I yield to no one in my contention that Les Ames was the greatest wicketkeeper/batsman of all. Alan Knott has an obvious claim to that title, having made 4,389 Test match runs with his blend of skill and guts, flexibility and sheer audacity. Yet Ames in less than half as many Test innings scored eight centuries and averaged over forty.

A natural athlete who played professional football on the wing, Ames had the lightest footwork which helped to make him a magnificent opponent of spin. I never saw a batsman more consistently set on confronting slow bowlers from so far down the pitch. Add to his batting the unobtrusive, ever-efficient manner in which he gathered in his host of victims – whether standing up to 'Tich' or a long, long way back to Larwood and Voce on the 'Bodyline' tour – and the overall record is peerless of its kind.

The younger generation tend to think we old 'uns go on over-much about times past. Yet when I am asked to compare England's overall batting strength in recent years with what I remember from long ago, I like to make the point that Geoff Miller, a highly respected all-rounder, appeared in his country's middle order without ever having made a first-class hundred. Les Ames very rarely batted higher than No. 7 for England, but he is one of the immortal gallery who made more than a century of centuries.

A dinner in honour of his eightieth birthday was held at the St Lawrence ground in Canterbury last December. I was

163

thrilled to be asked by Kent's chairman, John Pocock, to join Godfrey Evans and 'Hopper' Levett on the toast list and, as a souvenir of the occasion, I have a photograph of four wicketkeepers whose combined skills no county has ever matched. Les wears his years wondrously lightly and still plays his golf (72 holes a week) to a handicap of 15.

It is a great deal easier, as captains at all levels may agree, to lead a strong and winning side rather than an indifferent losing one. David Gower would have echoed this truth when first thrust into the England captaincy with little or no experience of leadership on the field (which was not his fault). It certainly showed when he first took charge of the Test side. Yet no one ever suggested that Norman Yardley was a poor captain after England had lost the Test series to Don Bradman's great Australian team in 1948 by a margin, 4-0, almost as conclusive as the whitewash Gower's side suffered at the hands of Clive Lloyd's West Indians in 1984. When he took over the English reins Yardley had learned his captaincy trade at school, university, county and higher levels. Gower had enjoyed no such background, but there were encouraging signs in 1985 that he was getting to grips with a testing job.

I rate Bradman, Benaud, Illingworth, Ian Chappell and Brearley as the outstanding post-war Test captains, with New Zealand's Geoff Howarth coming close. Of all these the best, I think, were Benaud and Brearley, and I am content to accept Jim Laker's opinion that Benaud was the finest captain he played with or against. To Benaud's knowing and lively gifts on the field was added a journalist's shrewd capacity for dealing with the media, a skill, which some captains see as a mandatory chore, rarely equalled and certainly not bettered since.

With carrot or whip the subtle, thoughtful Brearley enjoyed the priceless ability in a captain of being able to inspire an individual to do his best. What is more, he had the respect of Ian Botham and with the unerring touch of a

164

psychoanalyst knew exactly how to play the joker in his pack. I am tempted to bracket Raymond Illingworth alongside Benaud and Brearley, with both of whom he shared a mastery of every tactical nuance, but there was something of Len Hutton's native caution in his make-up and his approach was sometimes rather too defensive. I did not see Keith Fletcher at England's helm in India in 1981–2, but I thought him subsequently unlucky to lose the Test leadership. Since Brearley's retirement he has been by some way the best of our county captains.

Although not choosing Clive Lloyd as one of the outstanding tacticians of my time, I am in no doubt at all about putting this benign, avuncular man in my list of great fieldsmen. Patrolling the covers in his prime with catlike tread, he was remarkably swift and athletic for a big man and his throwing off-balance could be as dramatic, though not perhaps so often as lethally accurate, as that of South Africa's Colin Bland.

As a fielder anywhere, and especially to his own bowling, Learie Constantine was, and I use the word advisedly, sensational. That lovable character, Derek Randall, has made the same sort of spectacular impact. In his more pragmatic but no less effective fashion, Neil Harvey as a cover-point or all-round practitioner must go into my eclectic list. Alan Davidson was another outstanding fielder for Australia.

I did not see Walter Hammond, much less Frank Woolley, in their prime at slip but what I observed in their declining years was good enough for me. Keith Miller, pausing briefly from a conversation with a colleague and languidly withdrawing hands from pockets, was one of the great performers in that position. For polished consistency there surely can have been no one better at first slip than Bobby Simpson. Of those who stand wider I can't believe that anyone has been better than Ian Botham. Moreover, he stands closer to quick bowling than anyone else.

The old orthodox position of backward short leg to the quicker bowlers seems to have gone out of favour. Tony

Lock distinguished it in his heyday with some marvellous catching, one example of it, off the bowling of Frank Tyson at the Oval, remaining clear in my memory after more than thirty years. Day in and day out, I doubt if any team had a better close catcher on the leg side than Glamorgan's Peter Walker, who played three times for England in 1955.

The bravest – and perhaps most reckless – close fielder I ever saw was Brian Close, who would stand almost in the batsman's hip pocket at short square leg. There were no helmets in those days and, if there had been, Close would have spurned one – just as Phil Edmonds does, stationed equally adjacent in the present era.

Chapter Eight

As well as enabling an aspiring commentator to cut his teeth at the cricket, the old B.B.C. West region provided him with opportunities to talk in the winter about the other great love of his sporting life. By the time Basil Kenyon's fourth Springboks team from South Africa came to play South West Counties on the Plymouth Albion football ground in 1951, a promising young broadcaster named Alan Gibson was also ready for his introduction to rugby commentary. It did not in fact last very long: he was taken ill during the first half and whisked off to hospital. So I was left to talk non-stop throughout the last forty minutes of the contest.

After that initial hiccup Alan made his mark as a broadcaster far beyond the confines of rugby and cricket. For the past thirty years and more he has also delighted a host of readers with the rich quality of his essays and his off-beat, not to say eccentric, match reports. I have always admired and envied his unusual talent. He is the only man I know who can devote the early paragraphs of his cricket account in *The Times* to his troubles on British Rail, most of them when changing trains at Didcot, or the latest gossip from the barmaid in the members' room at Bristol. Apart from all this he has been a trusted companion at the microphone, and I regret that it is a long time since we were able to work together.

My experiences as a rugby commentator on sound radio

in the late forties and early fifties were limited, just as they had been on cricket, by the opportunities presented in a different medium. I did my first television rugby commentary in 1949 and my last, eighteen seasons later, when Wales lost at home to France in 1968. They were not to lose another championship match in Cardiff until Scotland's handsome victory there, fourteen years on, in 1982.

With the limited technical resources then at his disposal in the old days of black and white television, Antony Craxton brought to his production of rugby the same artistry which characterized his direction of cricket. For most of those early years my respected companion in the commentary box was Michael Henderson, who had won a war-time Blue for Oxford in 1939. It was a long time before the B.B.C. introduced a third voice, in the person of an old international, for 'inter-round' summaries. One of the first of these was Cliff Morgan, who joined the Corporation in Cardiff after his brilliant playing career was done, then moved on to London to take charge of 'Grandstand' and other big sports programmes. Eventually, after a productive stint as head of Outside Broadcasts (Radio), he returned to television in a similar capacity. Of all the old players I have heard speaking at rugby dinners I have known no one to match Cliff Morgan for his capacity to hold an audience in the palm of an emotive hand – and no one more impassioned in upholding the ethos of a hard, body-contact game in which there has to be a clear distinction between what is fierce and honourable and what is sordid and unacceptable.

The longer I lasted as a television rugby commentator the more I had to realize that, on account of all the other programmes with which I was involved, I was walking on a tightrope. A glance at an old diary reveals that in the course of a fortnight I did duty at two rugby internationals, completed a week's stint on 'Housewives' Choice' and anchored four other programmes, namely 'Get Ahead', 'Going to Work', 'Meeting Point' and 'Come Dancing'. The last of these provided an obvious stick for some of the rugby fraternity to belabour the hapless commentator. This Sassenach endured a steady stream of abuse from Scotland – though significantly none at all when Bill McLaren joined me in the commentary box for Calcutta Cup games – and, to a lesser extent, from Wales. But the writing looked to be on the wall when a banner, paraded in front of the cameras at Twickenham, proclaimed that Peter West should stick to 'Come Dancing'.

At the same time I was not always able, because of my other commitments, to do all the essential homework in advance of the rugby matches. The result was an occasional mistake in the identification of players, and I have to admit, in retrospect, that for whatever reasons my approach to it was not professional enough. I could not feel surprised to be superseded by Bill McLaren, although I was disappointed to be dropped without anyone, least of all the rugby producer, Alan Mouncer, having the courtesy or courage to tell me about it. But after a season, as it were, on the touchline, it was a comfort to be asked by Jacob de Vries to revert to radio. I then clocked up another seventeen winters in a different capacity.

Even with an exclusive concentration on rugby I could not have matched the all-round qualities of Bill McLaren, a master of his TV craft. He is one of a rare breed who satisfies the knowledgeable viewers as well as those who appreciate some basic guidance. His identification of players in confused and sometimes confusing situations is wonderfully accurate, not simply because he has always been close to rugby but because in doing his homework he is a conscientious *nonpareil*. He has an encyclopaedic knowledge of the game. In his playing days he was good enough, shortly after the war, to get a trial for Scotland, but a serious illness put paid to his playing career. His impartiality is unquestioned. For many years he has regarded himself as a schoolmaster first, and a rugby commentator second. That must make him a remarkable instructor, and an inspiration to young folk in the Borders.

In the summer of 1971, when pledged to a further season of 'Come Dancing' in the following winter, a meeting with John Hennessy, then sports editor of *The Times*, led to a gratifying turn of events. He was looking for a new rugby correspondent following the retirement of Uel Titley, who had inherited the role from O. L. Owen, for many years the doyen of his profession. I was flattered to be offered the job and delighted to accept the challenge it provided. There was scope for a new man to broaden the paper's rugby horizons again by getting himself more often into the provinces where the heart of English rugby beats strongest.

I had a dozen happy and I hope productive years reporting rugby for *The Times* under three sports editors, John Hennessy, Nicholas Keith and, finally, Norman Fox. Of these, Keith was the only one who shared my passion for rugby but all sought to give me the space I asked for and at least I was able to say, 'Never mind the quality, feel the width.' There were days when I felt I would have been a lot better off being paid on a piece-work basis.

Reporters or feature writers blessed with ample space have an easier task than those required to compose much shorter pieces for the popular newspapers. It is more taxing to put together a coherent picture of a match in, say, 300 words, than it is at double the length. Those with a lot of column inches at their disposal have to guard against indisciplined writing, but the danger of this should be diminishing because match reports, even in the daily 'heavies', seem to be getting ever shorter. Today's rugby players would be surprised to pick up a pre-war newspaper and see how much space was devoted to an account of an international.

Many journalists may envy the talents of a Hugh McIlvanney, with his reports and essays in the *Observer*, or of an Ian Wooldridge, whose *Daily Mail* features, laced with wit and style, are, at their best, unmatched. Most of us are wise to settle for something more prosaic and within our compass.

Different readers no doubt require different things of their reporters. I am old fashioned enough to believe that most of them want at least to have the facts presented correctly and to feel when they read their paper (having been to a match) that they were at the same one as their reporter. Most of them seek enlightenment about what happened, how it happened and why it happened. A reporter must be expected to have his own opinions and to present them in a balanced and reasoned fashion. We all have prejudices, some of us more than others, but reporters should be careful not to let them intrude too much and to be flexible in their thinking, because form and circumstances can change.

We are all trying, I suppose, to be our own little window on the rugby world, seeking to inform and to entertain, but not at the expense of accuracy. There is always a danger that people in the media, just like those in high places, can take themselves too seriously. With a daily platform in print it is easy for correspondents to become dogmatic, all-knowing, and to believe they are composing regular holy writ. It is just as easy to think that everything is black or white when indeed the truth of the matter may be closer to a shade of grey. Happily, the players can be a useful safety valve for the deflation of reporters, just as reporters can have their uses when they come to deflate authority.

The Times was always a pleasant, accommodating paper to write for because, for the most part, a contribution thought to be adequately written to the length required was not hacked about on its way into print. It might, of course, be reduced in length to fit the space available in changing circumstances, and a correspondent could not complain about that. In common with my colleagues I had occasional cause for grievance when the sense was changed or a sub-editor, not well abreast of the rugby scene, failed to correct what should have been an obvious error.

Reporters, often working against the pressure of the clock, deserve – and mostly receive – the protection of their sub-editors from the most absurd of gaffes. This is an insurance that television and radio commentators, working on live programmes, can never have. It is something that carping press critics, with time to polish their phrases, seem willingly to forget.

I have mentioned elsewhere how strange things can happen to a report along the line from writer to print, and I dare say they may continue to do so even in an age when the reporter keys copy straight into his portable computerized transmitter. Using the old-fashioned telephone and going through direct to the copy-taker, a journalist needs always to be on the *qui vive* for possible hiccups. Lazily assuming that my meaning was clear, I once dictated to a lady typist in Gray's Inn Road that 'X' set a ball up for 'Y' and omitted to stress, in an additional note to the sports desk, that the word 'ball' was singular. The end-product next morning was enjoyed by my rugby friends.

In the old days, if there was a comma out of place in *The Times*, one could imagine the editor instituting a court of enquiry. In the turbulent seventies standards declined, copy was inadequately dealt with in the readers' department and literal mistakes in print proliferated, notably in the early editions. This malaise, I might add, has not been confined to *The Times*. But a long-held belief at Printing House Square that it should always be regarded as the paper of reliable record turned into a sick joke.

Laggard progress in Fleet Street in this technological age has done nothing to improve the service rendered by newspapers to their readers in the provinces. Edition times have been advanced to a stage, long now established, where readers of *The Times* in Bath, Bristol or Gloucester cannot often hope to read a report of a match played in their area and finishing by 8.30 p.m. the previous evening. The price of progress these days seems in many areas of public service to take the form of one step forwards, and several backwards.

Most readers have little notion about the pressures to which journalists are subject. They may or may not agree with their paper's stance but they take its production for granted, just as television viewers accept a programme without bothering to wonder how it was put together. Such an attitude is the consumer's reasonable prerogative. Yet those who enjoy reading about their sport on Sundays might now and then give thought to the problems of a reporter, his match finishing at 4.30 p.m., who is required to have his copy for the first edition finished on the final whistle. His running account of the game, written while it was being played, goes through on the wire at pre-set times. At the final whistle he hurriedly composes a paragraph or two to 'lead' his story. Reporters on daily newspapers face the same problems when covering matches played the evening before.

In such circumstances there is often no time to write or type the whole report. Indeed some journalists ad lib their entire piece on the telephone. Such flexibility demands a rather special talent allied, as its owners will concede, to a helpful copy-taker and sub-editor at the receiving end.

Just as films and television programmes have tended for many years now to begin with action preceding the opening titles – in order to hook their customers on what comes next – so sports reporters need their opening paragraphs to encapsulate the essence of the contest and encourage their customers to read on. I tended to spend a long time on a Sunday composing my lead for Monday morning's report. But nothing so concentrates the reporter's mind as the approach of a dreaded deadline, and I sometimes think one's best efforts can come off the cuff, as it were, when the adrenalin pumped by a good contest is still flowing freely.

One weekend task I held to be essential. If the match I was reporting for Monday's paper had been televised, I never failed to study the video recording. Sunday's reporters can be excused for occasional errors of fact, although on the big occasions these days there are television screens in the press boxes. Monday's scribes have no such excuse.

I suppose I might still be writing for *The Times* were it not for several unforeseen developments. Because of my television cricket commitments to the B.B.C. in the summer, it was understood from the outset at Printing House Square that I would be unable to cover Lions' tours for the paper. I thus had to forgo the Lions' triumphant expedition to South Africa in 1974. None the less, *The Times* did dispatch me to cover three short England tours – to Australia in 1975, to Japan, Fiji and Tonga in 1979 and to Argentina (a year before the Falklands conflict) in 1981.

By the time the Lions toured again, in New Zealand in 1977, I was so determined to accompany them on behalf of my paper that I was prepared to miss a whole season of cricket – and run the evident risk of endangering a further commitment with B.B.C. Television. At the last moment *The Times* declared that for reasons of economy they could not justify the expense of sending their rugby correspondent to New Zealand. This notwithstanding the fact that every other national newspaper except one was sending its man on the trip. I found it hard to understand how a newspaper purporting to take rugby seriously could leave its rivals to cover the tour in depth, and settle instead for taking humdrum and quite inadequate agency reports from overseas. It was galling to be left behind, but I lived with the disappointment until, six years later, the Lions were due in New Zealand again.

In the winter of 1982, with the blessing of my then sports editor, Nicholas Keith, I threw myself on the mercy of B.B.C. TV's head of sport, Jonathan Martin. To cover the 1983 Lions tour of New Zealand, I said, would fulfil one of my greatest ambitions. Would he agree to release his cricket anchorman from his contract? His reaction, in all the circumstances, was understanding and generous. Yes, he would – provided I was available to the B.B.C. for the two-and-a-half weeks of cricket's World Cup in June 1983. This would entail me missing one of the Lions' four international matches in New Zealand.

Back then, I went, to my sports editor. I would be prepared, I told him, to fly home from New Zealand and then back again, for the rest of the rugby tour, at my own expense. Yes, that would be acceptable. So all, I thought, was arranged. But yet again *The Times* declined to send me. The editor, Charles Douglas-Home, pulled up the drawbridge just as he had done, in a different capacity, six years earlier. I think every other national paper sent their man to New Zealand on this occasion. The economic difficulties cited once more by my editor had not precluded *The Times* from sending Richard Streeton to cover the early part of England's cricket tour in Australia, or dispatching their highly respected cricket correspondent, John Woodcock, for the last months of it. It seemed to me there was one law for the Medes and another for a wretched Persian. All in all, I took this latest disappointment to be the last straw. I resigned from *The Times* and went back cap in hand to a sympathetic Jonathan Martin to ask if the B.B.C. would undo the arrangements being made for my temporary absence the following summer.

My decision to resign was influenced by several other factors, one of them being that the paper was so far in arrears with its monthly payments to a free-lance contributor that it owed me more than £3,000. I dare say I would not have made it had I been wholly dependent on Mr Rupert Murdoch for a living. Such gestures are often futile, but I still believe I was justified in doing what I did. I ought to add that after my departure *The Times* was soon putting many thousands on its circulation – a case perhaps of cause and effect. On, I hope, a more serious note it was plain that the paper's new-found popularity at that time was based to a considerable extent on the innovations wrought by Harold Evans during his brief though traumatic tenure as editor.

My long association with B.B.C. Radio as a rugby commentator came to an abrupt halt at the end of 1985 in circumstances which left me feeling distinctly hard done by. Having played a leading part in the rugby output for seventeen years, and having at no time received any indication that any change in my status was contemplated, or that I had ever fallen short of the standards required, I received, barely four weeks before the international season began, a firm invitation to commentate on just one championship match and one Barbarians fixture at Easter. I wrote to tell them that I thought the offer, which I declined, was a derisory one. The subsequent letter, kindly but, I felt, unconvincingly phrased, did little to assuage my indignation. I remained convinced that the matter could have been handled in a more sensitive fashion. It would never have happened like that in the old days.

To an often-posed question 'Which sport, cricket or rugby, is your favourite one?' I always give the answer, 'Cricket in the summer, rugby in the winter.' I have been equally potty about the two games since I first learned the pleasure of running with a ball in my hands and tackling boys bigger than myself. If there are few sights more unrewarding than a poor game of rugby union football it is surely equally true to suggest that the game at its best presents the most exhilarating spectacle. It calls for courage, high skills and a selfless approach. It is essentially a team game and you will not see many examples – as you would in cricket – of one man turning or winning a match virtually on his own. It is also a game which can be played badly by its participants and still be enjoyed. It ought not to be forgotten that whereas at its more exalted levels the participants get fit to play rugby, at the other end of the scale thousands of players are taking part every weekend in order to have fun and keep fit.

I saw my first international in 1933, when their captain, Watkyn Thomas, inspired Wales to a first victory at Twickenham after nine previous failures. In the Welsh back division two young University players were blooded at international level: Vivian Jenkins (Oxford) and Wilfred Wooller (Cambridge). Under the laws of rugby then in force Vivian Jenkins, who was strong, brave, resourceful and armed with a very effective boot, struck me as being the

176

beau ideal of a full-back. Wilfred Wooller, standing well over six feet and weighing in at over fourteen stone, was a most formidable, aggressive runner: an outstanding centre who, sadly for the British Isles team, was unable to tour South Africa in 1938. I am glad I never had to mark him, and I have the same sentiments about Claude Davey, his partner in the Welsh centre that day, who crash-tackled his opponent round about the rib cage – just as his compatriot, Jack Matthews, did in the immediate post-war era. Many years later I enjoyed working with Wilfred Wooller on televised cricket in Wales. A big and fearless man, his trenchant views have not endeared him to everybody but when the shot and shell are flying I would always want him on my side.

In the Welsh international at Twickenham in 1935 I had sight of Cliff Jones whose dazzling, side-stepping running left such an indelible impression on my memory that I have always rated him one of the great stand-off halves. Three years later, when Scotland clinched the Triple Crown with a spectacular victory, 21-16, at Twickenham, I saw another. No wonder this encounter came to be known as Wilson Shaw's match. With breathtaking pace and swerve the Scottish stand-off scored two of Scotland's five tries, the last of them sealing the result. Who could have thought then that Scotland would wait another forty-six years before winning the Triple Crown again?

In January 1936 I had also been lucky enough to see at Twickenham the first victory that England achieved against New Zealand in this country. This was another match which afterwards became linked with the name of one man, Prince Obolensky, whose two tries for England have been pre-served for posterity in newsreel black and white. Almost fifty years later, on the eve of a second English success against New Zealand at Twickenham, I was able on behalf of the *Daily Telegraph* to bring together in Cambridge most of the survivors of the 1936 side. These were the captain and scrum-half, Bernard Gadney; the leader of the pack, Major-General Douglas ('Joe') Kendrew, who won four DSOs in the war and subsequently became Governor-General of Western Australia; two more forwards in Dr Edward Nicholson (hooker) and Bill Weston (flanker); and two threequarters, Peter Cranmer and Hal Sever. There were three more survivors, but the full-back, 'Tuppy' Owen-Smith, was in South Africa, and the stand-off, Peter Candler, in Nairobi. Another forward, 'Pop' Dunkley, was traced, too late, in county Durham.

The second and more spectacular of Obolensky's tries, when he cut inside and scythed a blistering path through a wrong-footed defence, is the one that subsequently received star billing. Yet it was the unanimous opinion of those gathered at Cambridge that Obolensky, a wing with little instinctive ball sense, just kept running for that try without any clear idea where he might finish up. They all thought that his first try, when he went outside the New Zealand full-back with a devastating swerve and change of pace was, for the purist, a finer effort.

Prince Alexander Obolensky was born in Petrograd in 1916. When England wanted him in their rugby XV in 1936, I believe he was given British citizenship even more quickly than Zola Budd about forty years later. He won four caps, all of them in 1936, joined the RAF at the outbreak of war and as a pilot officer lost his life on a night training flight in 1940. It was touching to hear from Bernard Gadney that shortly before he came to meet his old playing colleagues in Cambridge he had left a poppy on Obolensky's grave at Martlesham, near Ipswich. 'I put it there', he said, 'from all of us.'

Of the two university matches I saw while I was at school I retain vivid memories of an incident in 1937 when Cambridge were hotly fancied to win. They had a redoubtable midfield trio comprising R. B. Bruce-Lockhart, J. G. S. Forrest (both later to play for Scotland) and W. H. Roden. Oxford therefore chose to play their South African full-back, H. D. Freakes, in the centre, where it was planned that he should clatter Forrest at the first time of asking. This he did with a tremendous tackle which seemed to reverberate around the stands. Forrest simply got ball and man together, and was badly shaken up. An inflexible Cambridge side persisted in spreading the ball wide; the Oxford back row, P. K. Mayhew outstanding, came more and more into its own. Oxford scored five tries in winning by 17 points to 4. The Rev Owen Chadwick, now Regius Professor of Modern History at Cambridge, hooked for two winning teams at Twickenham but was on the losing one then. 'A disaster,' he recalls. 'It never pays to underestimate the opposition.'

'Trilby' Freakes, who was to win three England caps (at full-back), and Johnny ('Springy') Forrest both lost their lives in the war. Forrest, a brilliant runner with an extremely deceptive sidestep, had time to share in Scotland's Triple Crown and 'Wilson Shaw's match' at Twickenham when he played on the wing. The two fine Scottish centres that day were Charles Dick and Duncan Macrae.

It is a measure of the consistent power and skills of New Zealand rugby that their loss to England at Twickenham in 1936 is one of only 15 defeats they have suffered in 234 matches in these islands, whether on major tours or on expeditions to one or more of the home countries. I was four years old when Colin Porter's second All Blacks proved invincible in 1924–5, George Nepia playing in all of their twenty-eight matches, but a lot older in the tooth when I met him on a recent tour of Wales. Of all my feature pieces in *The Times* few gave me more pleasure than the one I wrote about this prince of full-backs.

I was not a witness when Swansea with their schoolboy half-backs, Haydn Tanner and Willie Davies, and Wales, with Tanner and Cliff Jones, brought down Jack Manchester's team in 1935–6. But since the day when England won at Twickenham that season, I have seen every defeat of the All Blacks in the British Isles.

I saw Bleddyn Williams lead Cardiff to an 8-3 victory over Bob Stuart's side of 1953–4, and then lead Wales to another,

179

by 13-8, when a famous cross kick from Clem Thomas led to the try by Ken Jones which clinched the result. Cliff Morgan and Rex Willis at half-back, and Gareth Griffiths at threequarter, were three distinguished backs who shared in those successes. I was in the TV commentary box on both occasions, just as I was, ten years later, when Wilson Whineray's fifth All Blacks side suffered their only defeat, at the hands of Newport, on a filthy afternoon at Rodney Parade. The only score in a fierce and desperately close encounter was a dropped goal by Dick Uzzell. Resilience and discipline did the trick for Newport: Don Clarke, a mighty goal-kicker, was given no chances. Glyn Davidge, heroic in the rucks as Newport's No. 8, must have carried his battle scars for weeks afterwards.

One of my happiest memories of that tour was to talk excitedly on TV about the try Whineray scored at the climax of their spectacular 36-3 victory over the Barbarians. The opposing defence had been spreadeagled when the All Blacks' captain dummied under the posts to a thunderous ovation. At the end of it all the two teams linked arms while the crowd sang 'Now is the hour' with a warmth and a fervour I have not heard equalled since.

There were no All Blacks' defeats for any of us to witness when, apart from a 3-3 draw with East Wales in Cardiff, Brian Lochore's team on a short tour in 1967 marched invincibly through three of the home countries – and France for good measure as well. This New Zealand side was so well armed in every respect that it has a strong claim to being regarded as the best of all post-war touring sides in these islands. The mighty Colin Meads, then at his peak, was at the heart of a pack which spilled back gilt-edged, second-phase ball like a duck laying eggs, and Chris Laidlaw with his swift and accurate service was not a scrum-half to waste it.

New Zealand scored four tries in the first half against England with as clinically efficient an exhibition of rugby as I have seen. Had they toured Ireland, I do not doubt they

would have achieved the Grand Slam which Graham Mourie's All Blacks were to pull off in 1978. But I remember what
a close call Lochore's men had against an East Wales side
which included Barry John and Gareth Edwards at half-
back, Gerald Davies and John Dawes in the centre and Ken
Jones on a wing.

The All Blacks side of 1972–3, led by Ian Kirkpatrick, was
held to a draw by Ireland, beat the other home countries
but, unprecedentedly, lost four times in other matches. It
was not a happy tour, most notably in Wales where the rival
camps seemed to bring out the worst in each other. The
New Zealand prop, Keith Murdoch, was sent home following an affray in a Cardiff hotel. By their graceless behaviour
in public some of the senior All Blacks players – not their
fine captain, I hasten to say – added nothing to the amity
between nations. A lot of bridges were left for mending
when the side flew home.

Matters were conducted in a more acceptable fashion on
the field when Llanelli were the first to bring the tourists
down. The supercharged atmosphere of that day at Stradey
Park will be etched for ever in my memory. The blueprint
for victory was prepared by Carwyn James, whose coaching
of the British Lions in New Zealand in 1971 had played so
vital a part in their historic success. An inspired Llanelli side
put it into practice with a stunning result which was
rightfully earned.

The captain, Delme Thomas, Derek Quinnell, an
immense ubiquitous force, the flanker, Tom David, and the
prop, Barry Llewelyn, were the best known names amongst
eight forwards who were heroes all. There were no irresistible drives that day by the All Blacks' loose forwards, who
were knocked over by conclusive tackling. Behind the
scrummage Llanelli had Phil Bennett at stand-off half, Roy
Bergiers and Ray Gravell in the centre, J. J. Williams on one
wing and Andy Hill, a prolific scorer of points, on the other.
When Hill kicked a penalty, the last points of the game, to a
noise that might have been heard across the Bristol Chan-

nel, the scoreboard read: 'Llanelli 9, Seland Newydd 3'. Ten minutes remained. I looked round from the press seats at the All Blacks' manager and coach behind me. Their faces were an ashen grey as they saw the writing on the wall. At no-side both teams were engulfed by an ecstatic crowd, and Delme Thomas was chaired in triumph from the field. 'We went out to die for the cause,' Carwyn James said, 'and we did.'

Three weeks later, on another red-blooded day, North West Counties became the first English combination, aside from the national XV, to beat an All Blacks team. With rain squalls driving over the Workington ground's gaunt industrial setting and the steelworks spewing their smoke down a bitter wind, the Counties prevailed 16-14 thanks to a latish try in which two of their illustrious forwards, Fran Cotton (the captain that day) and Tony Neary, played a crucial part. A third England forward in the ranks was Peter Dixon. All three of them were to share, seven years later in 1979, in another even more significant victory over a team from New Zealand. A young Steve Smith played at Workington with outstanding resource at scrum-half. For the players and for their coach, John Burgess, it was one of their finest hours.

By then Kirkpatrick's tourists had been revealed as predictable and clearly beatable. They squeezed home 19-16 by the odd penalty goal in their first international, against Wales, but then lost again, to Midland Counties (West), on Moseley's ground at the Reddings. The margin, 16-8, was conclusive enough. I retain a special memory of a try by Martin Cooper, who was to be capped a season later as England's stand-off half. On this occasion he was on the left wing, and the score he got was a classic of its kind.

David Duckham, who was to become the most capped of all England's backs, led the Midlands to that victory and at the end of that All Blacks' tour had a brilliantly telling hand in their fourth defeat. 'Even hardened critics,' I wrote in *The Times*, 'could scarce forbear to stand and cheer as the tour came to its spectacular finish in a blaze of running rugby. It was a victory not just for the Barbarians, 23-11, but for the game itself.' New Zealand's manager, Ernie Todd, observed afterwards that the Barbarians took the prime fleece while his side ended up with the crutchings. 'We salute the Barbarians,' he said, 'for their champagne football.'

After so generous a tribute I suggested in my report that it would not come amiss for everyone in these islands to salute Ian Kirkpatrick and his team for entering totally into the spirit of the occasion, and for keeping Sid Going on the field for as long as they did. Having spent the first quarter of the game spinning out a sumptuous service, Going's suspect ankle slowed his footwork and contributed crucially to two of the Barbarians' tries. Their first, rounded off by Gareth Edwards with an irresistible surge from 35 metres out – after Phil Bennett with a swerve and two dazzling sidesteps in his 22 had sparked off a marvellous move involving seven pairs of hands – has passed into legend. But, looking at the whole match, the breathtaking running of David Duckham out of defence must, in my book, run it close in the honours list.

Graham Mourie's All Blacks of 1978 pulled off an historic Grand Slam against the four home countries, but they lost to Munster in Limerick, and I rejoiced to be there to see a piece of history of a different sort. With that *furor Hibernicus* familiar to almost all touring sides who visit the southernmost province, Munster fashioned a rousing 12-0 victory and thus became the first side to beat the All Blacks on Irish soil. 'Immortal they'll be,' Ned van Esbeck of the *Irish Times* confided to me in the press box. 'I'll swear it.'

Having been thankful to beat Ireland with a late try in an unmemorable encounter, Mourie's team must then have been even more relieved to gain the narrowest of verdicts over Wales. They won in Cardiff 13-12, and Houdini himself might not have sprung the Welsh trap to better effect. Wales indeed were leading 12-10 with five minutes left when a penalty awarded against them at a lineout gave New Zealand's substitute full-back, McKechnie, the chance to save the day. That he took it, with a perfect kick under intense pressure, stands greatly to his credit.

Much less creditable were the goings-on at that lineout to which Wales had the throw. I quote from my report. 'As Windsor threw in the ball for Wales, Haden, the New Zealand lock, though untouched by an opponent, fell out of the lineout with an histrionic lurch that might win him nomination for an Oscar but certainly no honour in rugby terms. It was Wheel, palming back for Wales at number two, who was apprehended by Mr Quittenton for, as the referee said afterwards, "climbing upon an inside shoulder".'

It is not always easy for an Englishman to feel sorry for Wales, particularly one who has crept away, humiliated, from Cardiff after a succession of English disasters there. On that occasion I was in a distinct minority, outside of the principality, in thinking them hard done by. As Wheel jumped to palm the ball back with his right hand, his left shoulder brushed against his opposite number, Oliver, who was bent, in a less overt way, on repeating what Haden had done. I have great respect for the refereeing of Roger Quittenton, then handling his first international, but I believe that in this instance he made a mistake. However, it behoves everyone to live with a referee's decisions. The Welsh rugby fraternity won no marks for the manner in which Quittenton was subsequently pilloried.

Back now to those matches lost by the All Blacks, and to one in which they suffered their biggest defeat anywhere in these islands. This was the fate of Mourie's second touring side when England's Northern division won a tremendous victory at Otley, in 1979, by 21-9. More significantly, perhaps, the North scored four splendid tries from relatively close range; on a dirty afternoon made to measure for their endeavours, everything worked out just as the coach, Des Seabrook, the captain, Bill Beaumont, and his senior players had planned. The inspiring Beaumont was one experienced addition in the pack to three old hands, Cotton, Neary and Dixon, who had shared in the Workington victory of 1972.

Another, Roger Uttley, now joined Neary and Dixon to
form a loose forward trio whose contribution was immense.

At scrum-half there was Steve Smith, another survivor
from Workington, whose judgement was faultless. At
stand-off there was Alan Old, a player's player conducting
affairs with aplomb, having a crucial part in two of the tries
and scoring one himself. The wholehearted centre, Tony
Bond, got a brace of them. Mike Slemen was on one wing
and John Carleton, about to win his first England cap, on
the other. After that utterly conclusive success by the
Northern XV there were no places for Uttley, Dixon or Old
when the national selectors named their side for the international shortly afterwards. England lost to New Zealand at
Twickenham by 10-9. Yet within a few months they had
won their first Grand Slam since 1957, and Uttley played a
regular part in that long-awaited triumph.

I have two more All Blacks' defeats to complete my list but
pleasure at their recollection must be tempered by the
knowledge that Stuart Wilson captained a touring side in
1983 which arrived in Britain without their leading locks and
front row men. Peter Wheeler led the Midlands division to a
rousing win, 19-13, at Leicester and then led England, in the
international, to a 15-9 victory. Under the lights at Welford
Road Dusty Hare clinched the first of these games with a
penalty from just inside his own half and a dropped goal,
just as prodigious but more unexpected, from about the
same distance. At Twickenham, where shrewdly they kept
attacking close-in, England achieved a pragmatic victory
heartening enough to suggest more prosperous times
ahead. Yet in the new year's championship they finished
one from bottom, their only success having been achieved
against Ireland who ended up, whitewashed, with the
wooden spoon. It was clear by then that the most senior
members of 'Dad's Army', which had brought Ireland the
championship title in 1982, and a share of it with France a
year later, were due for honourable pensions.

*   *   *

They were dizzy, all too briefly dizzy days for England when William Blackledge Beaumont led them to a Grand Slam, their first in twenty-three years, in 1980. It was a success built under the coach, Mike Davis, on an outstanding pack of forwards. That championship marked the end of their international road for the two flankers, Roger Uttley and Tony Neary, who was the most capped of all England players with forty-three.

Beaumont was rightly rewarded with the captaincy of the British Lions touring South Africa the following summer. The front row of Fran Cotton, Peter Wheeler and Philip Blakeway went there with him, as well as the massive lock Maurice Colclough whose form in the Republic reached an apogee not consistently matched for England afterwards. Uttley had been a member of the Lions' greatest pack in South Africa in 1974. Recurring back troubles must have cost him another visit to those parts. They almost certainly deprived him of the captaincy of the Lions in New Zealand in 1977.

Some alarming chest pains made Cotton's second Lions tour of South Africa a short one. Within months they had manifested themselves again in the first championship match of 1981, in Wales. That spelled the end of another distinguished career. A year later, after sustaining a head injury – by no means his first one – in a county game, Beaumont had to call it a day on medical advice, and almost certainly to miss the unique distinction of leading a second Lions side (to New Zealand) in 1983. Wheeler, Colclough and John Scott, the No. 8, soldiered on until the end of the 1984 championship. After that, Blakeway was the sole survivor of a Grand Slam pack the break-up of which marked a return to familiar lean times for England. Before the end of the 1985 championship he too had retired from the game on medical advice.

Beaumont captained his country a record nineteen times. That number excludes two matches against Argentina in Buenos Aires in 1981, when I was able to report some

examples of his selfless, inspiring leadership. England drew
the first international and won the second with as resilient
and committed a performance as I have seen from a side
wearing the white jerseys.

Apart from a brief sojourn in Cordoba, where the con-
tours of the landscape offered some variety, the English
party left Argentina with a conviction that the country was
distinctly flat. On a long train journey to the coastal city of
Mar del Plata the only undulations on an interminable plain
seemed to be mole hills. But there was nothing humdrum
about the hospitality extended by their rugby hosts which
matched in spirit and other practical ways the atmosphere
back home. We all had a splendid day at an *estanzia* where
an invitation to ride the local steeds was not, in my case at
least, accompanied by the warning that pulling on the reins
in Argentina was the green light for go. It may have looked
impressive as my horse galloped past the England team's
management, but its elderly rider was near to panic and
how he got the noble brute to revert to a decorous canter he
stiil doesn't know.

As well as writing for *The Times* I was committed on this
tour to sending home brief match reports and features for
B.B.C. Radio, on behalf of which I had a telephone conversation which may illustrate some of the difficulties experienced by correspondents in foreign fields. The England
players had experienced a sticky afternoon coping with a
regional team in Rosario, and emerged as unconvincing
winners only as the result of a late try superbly run in by
David Trick from out of his own half. The English press
fraternity was thankful to witness this remarkable score
since by then we were all mustered at a corner of the ground
behind the dead ball line, all set to catch taxis and late editions in Fleet Street (the time in Argentina is five hours
behind GMT). There were no local telephone facilities.

Before flying out from Heathrow I had been provided
with a schedule of radio requirements by Peter Baxter, who
genially presides over cricket's 'Test Match Special' and was

then the producer in charge of rugby. The list included a 45-second account of the said regional encounter for the late sports news at 10 p.m. This was not, I concede, an earth-shattering event but at least it offered rugby folk back home some tidings not otherwise available until they read their morning papers.

The Argentine telephone arrangements are not the country's most shining jewel. For twenty frustrating minutes, as I sought to get a call through, I felt an increasing conviction in my gut that I was about to miss a deadline. I knew only too well that those who habitually sit on news desks have little patience or understanding for the frust-rations of reporters overseas. But, praise be, the line came up in the nick of time, at 9.50 p.m. GMT, and the following conversation ensued.

'Good evening. This is Peter West with a short rugby report from Rosario for the sports desk.'

'Peter who?'

'Peter West.'

'From where?'

'From Rosario, Argentina.'

'What are you doing there?'

'I'm out here covering the England rugby tour, and I've got forty-five seconds for you on their match today.'

'What match?'

'England against the Littoral Region XV.'

'Against the what?'

'It doesn't matter. Let's just call it a local side. Can you take my copy because we're running out of time?'

'Well, we'll take it but it's not going to get in because we're already over the top with a lot of late football.'

So much for Peter Baxter's meticulous arrangements, duly communicated to all concerned.

This was also the tour on which two members of the side, Nick Jeavons and Steve Bainbridge, were arraigned before the players' court on a charge of sharing one brain and one hair dryer. The court was presided over by Mr Justice John

Fidler, a pillar of Gloucester and Gloucestershire rugby, then a PC in Cheltenham, who had been in the game a long time when at last he was deservedly capped in both internationals.

I have digressed from Bill Beaumont, whom I saw win all of his thirty-two caps for England. I certainly won't forget the day in Brisbane when he acquired his second, on England's short tour of Australia in 1975. That was an encounter in which, from the kick-off, the Wallaby forwards broke the rules of conventional rugby warfare and sparked off some general mayhem that was a disgrace to the game's image. As the fists flailed at the first lineout, the referee might have permed any two from sixteen forwards and dispatched them for an early bath. Shortly afterwards Mike Burton, for a late tackle, became the only Englishman to be sent off an international field. There were mitigating circumstances and we all felt relieved that his suspension from playing was relatively brief.

Beaumont had soon left the scene with a very nasty head wound requiring many stitches. But he came back and, moving up to prop in Burton's place, played a hero's part. It was clear that England had found a young forward of exceptional character. As a captain Beaumont was no tactical genius but he always led from the front. He had a lot in common with another Lancastrian, Eric Evans, who inspired England to their previous Grand Slam in 1957, and then, after being dropped by his county, led them to another championship title the following season.

It is sad that men with the sterling qualities of a Beaumont or a Fran Cotton can no longer play any official part in the game after writing a book about their experiences and retaining the profits. The day must surely come when the International Board permits players, *at the end of their careers*, to write one book for personal profit without surrendering their amateur status – provided it is held by the authority that what they write does not bring the game into disrepute. With such a dispensation the Beaumonts and Cottons could have looked forward to bringing their wisdom and special experience to coaching and administration. There are only a handful of players in any era with the charisma to interest the publishing trade.

I am not suggesting that an ex-player wishing to retain his amateur status should be allowed to make money from other activities connected with the game, such as journalism and broadcasting (unless it be his full-time activity), or be paid for making dinner speeches and opening shops. I support the fair and legitimate reimbursement of expenses to leading players whose commitment to the game has become an ever more time-consuming business, but I regard with dismay any suggestion that they should be paid to play. If that is what they want – and I am certain the vast majority of them do not – let them take up another game altogether.

When I sat down to write these pages on rugby I thought it would be of interest to discourse about the best players I have seen in all positions. Having then come to the conclusion that I would need another book to do the subject justice, I must content myself in the present covers with a selection at half-back.

Let me start with nine scrum-halves, five of them from the southern hemisphere and the rest from Wales. The oldest of them is Haydn Tanner, a Welsh maestro who won his first cap in 1935, his last in 1949, and thus lost too many of his finest rugby years to the war. He had all the right attributes for his position, not least a well-timed and powerful break. Then, in the fifties, came Onllwyn Brace. He won only nine caps for Wales and, not hitting it off with Cliff Morgan as his partner, played but one season in all four championship matches. His physique was on the frail side and no doubt he was at his best, as most scrum-halves tend to be, behind a winning platform at forward. But his play could be touched with genius – as anyone would confirm who saw him weaving innovative patterns with Mike Smith for Oxford University in 1955.

Gareth Edwards was not just the most capped (fifty-three for Wales, ten more for the Lions) of all scrum-halves but certainly as durable as any. He was as indestructible as Dick Jeeps for England and the Lions. His lethal strength close to his opponents' line has been equalled only by my fourth Welshman, Terry Holmes, whose career – in both codes – has been so disrupted by injuries. It may be that Holmes, with the physique of a flank forward, has been a touch more dangerous close-in, but Edwards was also a tactical kicker par excellence who frequently dictated where the game was to be played.

From South Africa, I pick one player, Dawie de Villiers – and can only wish that I had seen Danie Craven, for so long their rugby guru, in his heyday. From New Zealand I present three strong candidates, two of them with a special forte: Chris Laidlaw's was the speed and accuracy of an immaculate service, Sid Going's an unrivalled capacity to link effectively with the All Blacks' formidable loose forwards. Going could play a more expansive game if he wanted to – as his efforts testified in a great match against the Barbarians in 1973. More recently the All Black, Dave Loveridge, though not so physically robust as some scrum-halves, has possessed all the skills of their craft: he's a rounded, imaginative player, swift in thought and deed. And last, but certainly not least, I nominate the Australian, Ken Catchpole, whose lightning passes off either hand were such a joy to watch when the Australians toured Britain in 1966–7.

Catchpole did not kick a lot, but that was not the Australian way. He did it skilfully enough when necessary and, were I faced with the daunting challenge of picking an all-time, eclectic world XV within my own experience I would be hard pushed to decide whether to plump for him or Gareth Edwards. For all conditions and seasons my vote by a narrow margin goes to Gareth, and I do not suppose that South Africans who saw him reach his apogee, on the Lions' tour of 1974, would disagree with that verdict. Nor, come to that, the legions of the Welsh valleys.

191

As to the great stand-off halves, I have already remarked on the claims of players such as Cliff Jones and Wilson Shaw in the pre-war era. When Ireland won the Grand Slam in 1948, a Triple Crown in 1949 and then another championship in 1951 the man who orchestrated their successes was Jackie Kyle. He did a similar job for the Lions in New Zealand in 1950, but not, alas, behind a winning pack. There was not an aspect of Kyle's game which could be faulted. Kyle's international career, in which he collected a then world record number of caps (forty-six), spanned a dozen seasons and ended in the same one, 1958, as Cliff Morgan finished his days with Wales.

In Kyle's last international season the big, jovial Irish centre, Noel Henderson, then nearing the end of his road as well, scored a try against Australia from an interception and a long and painful run to the distant goal line. Was it true, he was subsequently asked, that a photographer got a shot of him receiving the pass and then another as he touched down? Noel gave the matter thought. 'Yes,' he said, 'and the bugger took his tripod with him.'

Cliff Morgan with his vivid acceleration and twinkling running was the archetypal Welsh stand-off and a player of very special charisma. He delighted to run with the ball but he was another who could kick, and kick to great effect, when he had to. I can remember him, one day at Twickenham, pushing his Welsh forwards up the touchlines with metronomic accuracy. Oh! to have been in South Africa in 1955 to see him run and serve a Lions' threequarter line which included Jeff Butterfield and Philip Davies at centre, and Tony O'Reilly on a wing.

In the fifties and sixties England had a succession of fine stand-off halves in men such as Martin Regan, Ricky Bartlett, Phil Horrocks-Taylor, Bev Risman and Richard Sharp. In the same era Scotland had another in Gordon Waddell. For a wet day, behind a struggling pack, I might pick any of these ahead of Richard Sharp, but he goes on my honours board for his attacking genius. In looks and style he epitomized the old ideas of what an England player in his position should be. Sharp's try against Scotland in 1963, when he scythed through the defence with a glorious outside break and a couple of dummies, must rank as one of the finest individual efforts I have seen. Twickenham, so often the graveyard for Scottish aspirations, was the stage for another remarkable though very different score two seasons later, when an unforgettable run by the left wing, Andy Hancock, from deep in his 22, saved England from a defeat they had deserved. He simply kept running, just beating a despairing Scottish cover defence to the corner. Some viewers north of the border thought my television commentary betrayed an obvious bias. It would have been difficult, I submit, to react in a low key.

But I got no brickbats when Peter Jackson won the match for England against Australia in injury time in 1958. That, too, was something to remember – a score seemingly conjured by the Coventry wing out of nothing. The magician himself modestly recalls that he just had room for manoeuvre. I have always thought that of the great wing threequarters Gerald Davies of Wales was the most consistently devastating runner-in of tries I have watched. But on his day Peter Jackson was peerless – a judgement confirmed by New Zealanders who saw him in action for the British Lions in 1959.

Since I have strayed off course on the subject of stirring individual scores I might as well mention two more. One was run in by Gareth Edwards for Wales against Scotland in 1972. Breaking irresistibly out of his 22, he chipped ahead over the full-back to win a charge for the ball and line with his face covered in reddish mud. Another memorable try was scored by the English centre, Clive Woodward, against Scotland (who seem almost always to be on the receiving end in these recollections) at Twickenham in 1981. A year earlier his incisive, creative running had made a shining contribution to the English victory at Murrayfield which clinched their Grand Slam – in an exhilarating match to which Scotland made handsome contribution with a thrilling recovery. Woodward's swerving, dummying run through a host of Scottish defenders in 1981 must surely rank with the finest of its kind. But I have digressed long enough from the subject of stand-off halves, amongst whom there stands the name of the Ulsterman, Mike Gibson.

In Gibson's second year at Cambridge I remember the university's rugby president, Dr Windsor Lewis, saying that he was quite simply the best player in his position he had ever seen. I agree with that judgement, for Gibson in his Cambridge and early Ireland days added to his remarkable gifts in attack the hardest defence of all his rivals. He seemed willing and able to confront an opposing pack on his own. But he finished his glittering, record-breaking career in the centre, where New Zealanders knew a great player when they saw one. I categorize him simply as the best *midfield* player of my time, and ease my problems, when choosing that world XV, by partnering him in the centre with Bleddyn Williams of Wales.

In the past two decades and more it has not been an unqualified pleasure for an Englishman to accompany the biennial rugby visit to Cardiff. A regular series of disasters was made harder to bear, at the peak of Welsh successes, by tactless remarks such as 'Boyo, if you don't improve, we'll have to drop the fixture.' Rugby folk in other countries unite in believing that it would be nice if the Welsh public as a whole could show more modesty in victory and, for that matter, a better grace in defeat.

There were precious few defeats in that purple or should I say scarlet Welsh era, beginning in the mid-seventies, when they won the championship four times in five years, including two Grand Slams and four successive Triple Crowns. By then, Barry John had retired at the peak of his career, following his triumphs with the Lions in New Zealand in 1971. Barry had little time for preconceived tactics and was bored by convoluted theories. 'Why not get the lads to let me have the ball in time,' he would say, 'and then I'll decide what to do with it.' All the best stand-off half-backs have a touch of arrogance about their play. This one was a supreme match-winner from hand or foot. A 'ghosting' runner, he inspired belief that he could walk the waters, and often did.

How blessed Wales were, when one great player had called it a day, to have another, Phil Bennett, to carry on the torch. Bennett's running in broken play was touched by genius. When he had retired – and before he was lured away by television in Wales – he contributed some very telling comments on the radio. For several seasons my vibrant partner on the air waves was Barry John, whose fame has never deterred him from showing a warm and genuine interest in people far less gifted than himself.

My final candidates at stand-off half come from the southern hemisphere. The Argentine, Hugo Porta, has been an admirably rounded player fit to rank with the greatest in his position: strong in shrugging off the tackle, remarkably elusive and penetrating at close quarters, and a masterly all-round kicker. On the Australians' last British tour Mark Ella's creative, one might almost say unique, genius in attack will not soon be forgotten. He had limitations as a tactical kicker but, there again, that was not the essential Wallaby style. Having chosen Mike Gibson in the centre for my world team I am left to choose a partnership at half-back to play in front of him. In all conditions of wind and weather and opposition, I choose Barry John and Gareth Edwards.

A few years ago Gareth Edwards and I were asked to entertain the company at a sporting dinner in the Midlands organized by Peter Robbins, a witty, highly accomplished speaker in his own right and an outstanding England flank forward in his day. I had never heard Gareth speak before, so subsequently I had to be very grateful to our host for knowing the form and getting my innings done with first. For an hour and more Gareth held 500 knowledgeable sportsmen spellbound with a riveting performance, the like of which I have heard equalled only by Cliff Morgan and Tony O'Reilly.

Run-of-the-mill speakers do well to discover in advance
what the proposed batting order is and then ensure they get
in before the star of the show. This I failed to do when invited
to sing for my supper at the centenary dinner of the Gala
rugby club, in the Scottish borders, which took place not long
after the British Lions of 1974 had returned from a triumphant
tour of South Africa. Their captain, Willie John McBride, got a
prolonged standing ovation at the end of his rousing speech.
We all know what follows the Lord Mayor's Show.

I remarked to the great O'Reilly once that I rarely got any
complaints from Irish viewers about my rugby commentaries. In my book, I said, Ireland were the best losers of all.
'That,' he replied, 'is because we get so much practice at it.'
Was it O'Reilly who declared that the state of English rugby
was serious but not hopeless, whereas that of Irish rugby was
hopeless but not serious? Some of my happiest hours have
been spent across the Irish channel, on both sides of the
border. North and south of it there remains a conviction that
however high the stakes, however important victory may be,
Kipling's twin impostors, triumph and disaster, should be
treated just the same.

I end some brief thoughts on rugby and its players with a
quite irrelevant story, which was told me by a member of the
Harlequins, about Denis Thatcher, an avid supporter of the
game and a county referee in his time. Mr Thatcher was the
guest of the club at their seven-a-side tournament in early
September. When it was all over and its social aftermath had
been enjoyed, he asked whether anyone might be able to give
him a lift back to Number 10. 'But surely,' my incredulous
informant said, 'you must have a government car?'

'No, I haven't,' Denis Thatcher replied. 'When I woke this
morning I said to Margaret, "I'm off this afternoon to a rugger
do." And she said, "Not that rugby again? We can't get the
chauffeur for that. Take the train." So I went to Waterloo and
came to Twickers. Now I can't remember where the bloody
station is.'

Conclusion

IT IS NO BAD moment, perhaps, to declare my innings closed as a presenter of cricket on television. I have covered Test matches in the medium for thirty-five summers and have worked for the B.B.C. on this or that for five years more. In another more invisible role I might have hoped to carry on for a few more seasons yet. But the B.B.C. needs a younger man to front the show.

It will be nice to spend more time with my wife, Pauline, who all these years has never wavered in her loyalty and support for an itinerant warbler so often away on the road. It will be just as rewarding to see more of our family. Jackie, our daughter (and eldest) and Will are town birds happily nesting with their two children, Nancy and Daniel, in Bristol. Our elder son, Simon, and his wife, Valerie, both work in that city but live in a handsomely converted old barn south of Bath. They have a young lad called Jonathan.

In order to be nearer to two-thirds of our tribe we settled, three years ago, on the outskirts of Duntisbourne Abbotts, a charming old village between Cirencester and Gloucester at the southern end of the Cotswolds. It was a great stroke of luck for us when, shortly afterwards, the youngest of our children, Stephen, and his wife, Sheila, came permanently to Cheltenham. They have two offspring, Kate and Timothy. We are a close-knit family and count our blessings.

Jackie, who got a First Class Honours degree in Sociology

197

at Exeter, has been a lecturer in that subject at Bristol University for sixteen years. Will is a BA in Philosophy at Exeter and a PhD in Sociology at Bristol. Simon, who read law at Newcastle, is a solicitor married to a solicitor and Stephen, who qualified at Guy's Hospital, is a GP married to an anaesthetist. Both of our sons wed beautiful girls, and we have never faulted their selection. They are shrewd observers of the cricket and rugby scene but their days as talented players were prematurely ended by the back troubles to which one side of the family is heir. It will be observed that all our three children are in the professions and thus a good deal more respectable than their father.

I shall now devote more time to gardening, a hobby to which I have become increasingly, the family say absurdly, addicted. I don't know a lot about it but I find even the more menial tasks to be therapeutic. I spend a fortune on fertilizers, weed and moss killers in ceaseless, hopeless pursuit of the perfect lawn. Thoughtful offspring gave me a magnifying glass last Christmas to enable the poor man's Percy Thrower to attack the smallest intruders on his sward.

It is a biggish garden, much bigger now than when we arrived in the Cotswolds, and I have certainly made a rod for a wonky back. But gentle exercise is useful, some healthy winds blow in the uplands and it all makes an admirable excuse for avoiding household chores. Gloucester rugby at Kingsholm is only twenty minutes away, that in Bath and Bristol not so very much further. Nowhere in England does the heart of rugby beat stronger. In the summer I shall spend more time watching the county of W. G. and Jessop, Hammond and (with respect to Worcestershire) Graveney. I shall enjoy spending more time with a buoyant Cheltenham Cricket Society, of which I am president. We have put down roots in a delectable neck of the woods, and I don't intend to leave it until I'm carried out feet first.

Postscript

OF THESE AFTERTHOUGHTS added at page-proof stage my first must be about the passing, within hours of each other, of Jim Laker and Bill Edrich. I heard the grievous news when taking another holiday with the Vennikers in Durban.

A fearless man of war and an indomitable cricketer, Bill in his three score years and ten had relished a good innings both on and off the field. Someone with his irresistible *joie de vivre* would have been pleased to hear that the stirring chords of *Jerusalem* were sung at his funeral, and that those attending it subsequently repaired to a local hostelry to toast his vibrant memory. I am sure he would be equally happy if I report that when he introduced us to his latest partner, he said: 'I'd like you to meet Mary. Fifth and final Test.'

On a further personal note I recall with gratitude the help Bill gave me when I edited the first *Playfair Cricket Annual*, in 1948. Gordon Ross, who took over that assignment in 1954, is another old friend of mine sadly no longer with us. Bill Frindall, recently established in the editor's chair, is an ideal person to preside over this popular and invaluable little *vade mecum*.

Jim Laker's qualities as a cricketer, commentator and raconteur I have already sought to describe. For twenty years and more Jim was a trusted colleague on television: a lovely, wryly humorous man whom we all held in affectionate esteem. Those of us in the commentary box – and a

199

host of viewers throughout the cricketing world – have lost a dear companion.

As to that recent, traumatic tour of the Caribbean, there cannot be much doubt that England with the battery of West Indian fast bowlers at their disposal would have won the series. It is noteworthy that in Shell Shield matches in Barbados, against Malcolm Marshall, Joel Garner and company, even the mighty Viv Richards averages less than 25. This speaks volumes for the effectiveness of a relentless pace attack and, to some extent no doubt, for a change in the Bridgetown pitch which Peter May, England's chairman of selectors, found to be very different from the one he last played on in 1959. But it was on the first Test pitch, in Kingston, with its lethal, unpredictable combination of lifters and shooters, that England's batsmen were unhinged at the first time of asking. I am sure that against that West Indian attack, on indifferent pitches, even the greatest players of yesteryear would have had a distinctly testing experience.

For one safely ensconced in an armchair 5,000 miles from torrid events it is easy to come to wrong conclusions. Television coverage here was very limited, the B.B.C. surely being justified in declining to pay, for more of it, the king's ransom demanded by an agent acting for the West Indies Board of Control. However, there were some much more extensive radio commentaries from Tony Cozier, Christopher Martin-Jenkins, Trevor Bailey, Geoffrey Boycott and all, and those of us enduring a nasty winter as well as an unspeakable early spring also had the benefit of printed reports from some respected correspondents. It was not just what happened on the field but what occurred – or failed to occur – off it that stuck in a pretty universal craw.

In this respect I submit the evidence of John Woodcock of *The Times*, who has covered something like thirty tours in nigh on forty years. 'Their [England's] practising,' he wrote, 'has been hopelessly inadequate and their training nothing like as hard as their opponents', and for that it is no good

blaming, as they do, the facilities. Much more imagination
could and should have been shown in making the best of
what was available, or finding something better . . . Never
have I seen such a lack of what the modern player so prides
himself in possessing – professionalism. That Tim Robinson
can lie for hours in the baking sun by the swimming pool on
the eve of a Test match, his energy being sapped by the
minute, is beyond comprehension. Why was he not
working on the obvious batting flaw which has been his
undoing? That Gower could go sailing when England were
losing their opening match, or that Neil Foster could bring
himself to saunter off for golf and others could go to the
beach when they had done nothing for several days after the
loss of the third Test match, is lamentable.'

When, in May, David Gower was reappointed as England
captain – initially for a brief tenure – John Woodcock had
this to say: 'In Barbados, after losing to the island side and
then by an innings to the West Indies, Gower made the next
practice, some days later, optional, and took himself off to
the beach. So much for the responsibilities which go with
leading England and for Peter May's injunction, earlier in
the week, that a special effort be made to "stop the rot". It
was this sort of thing, at least as much as Gower's tactical
shortcomings and the license he allows Botham, which
prompted the stern and timely warning . . . Then there was
Willis's failure to compensate for Gower's lack of commitment. To some extent those who appointed Willis to be
coach-cum-assistant manager sooner than was wise were
answerable for the ensuing humiliation, which was Gower's
own description of the tour. The fact remains, though, that
once again lip service, nothing more, has been paid to the
standards which the Board espouse yet which they know
are being compromised.

'Those standards have not least to do with appearances,
which means shaving more than every third day (those, that
is, without beards) and not looking like tramps or stretching
out on players' balconies in front of thousands of spectators

in only the briefest of shorts or being without blazers when meeting the Governor-General or taking the field in dribs and drabs. Such slovenliness was not to be seen last winter in the West Indian camp.'

Such strictures do not put the captain in the dock alone, but the management too. What was Bob Willis doing about it all, or the senior man, Tony Brown, at whose door the buck finally stops? It is true, as I allude to Woodcock's comments, that Peter May and the Test and County Cricket Board have administered a general rap on the knuckles and, by giving Gower the leadership for two Texaco Trophy matches and one Cornhill Test against India, have let it be known that the captain and his troops must get a corporate, wholly professional and responsible act together. But I think the selectors have hedged their bets. I think the time was ripe for a change of captain from the outset of a new English season.

My judgement of David Gower as a captain, so far as his tours are concerned, must be tempered by the knowledge that I did not see them at first hand. It is never easy to win in India, where he must have done a very adequate job. The same applies to his direction of affairs against Australia in 1985, when he had the pleasurable, and easier, experience of leading another successful side. When England were thrashed by the West Indies here in 1984 Gower, having only just been pitchforked into the captaincy, had looked a tyro whose tactical acumen alone left a great deal to be desired.

When England captains are compared, Gower must reflect ruefully that Mike Brearley, so generally held to be a master of his craft, never led England in a Test series against the West Indies. But the time surely had come, at the end of England's last tour of the Caribbean, for a change at the helm – for someone to crack the whip, to show a more positive approach.

That Gower can be casual to the point of flippancy has often been observed. He cannot have endeared himself to the selectors or the Board with the reported remark, 'What do they expect me to do, walk round in a T-shirt with "I'm in charge" on it?' I write these words knowing well that a 'laid back' leopard, changing his spots, may have got the message. If that be the case, it will certainly go down well in Leicestershire where, as I understand it, it has been difficult to motivate him to do much for his county off the field.

The overpoweringly successful Test cricket as now played by the West Indies is far removed from the game I was brought up to enjoy. Were it to become the general blue-print for winning at the highest level, the audience will not, I suspect, include those of a like mind; a countless host, who do not care for some of its essential parts. There may remain throughout the cricket world, in an age of changing tastes and values, a sufficient quorum of spectators who get a kick out of watching a constant fast attack, operating at such a miserable over rate that none of its members get tired. Yet even in the West Indies there must be many aficionados appalled by the sight of batsmen, padded and helmeted more and more like American footballers, struggling for runs, ducking and weaving to avoid grievous injury. There is now a consensus of opinion that the only way to beat the West Indies these days is to own four or five fast bowlers just as good, or at least just as intimidating. I shall be thankful not to be a commentator were this theory ever put to the test.

On the domestic scene, I think it is high time the Test and County Cricket Board prohibited players – as they used to do – from lending their names to press columns while they are touring with England teams. So-called exclusive revelations in one paper can spur its rivals to outdo them by dispatching *news* hounds whose brief has nothing to do with the cricket. It may be that by the time these words are read, the Board will have taken due action. It would be warmly supported by the great majority of sports editors.

Cricket this summer, thank the good Lord, will seem very different when England are confronted by India and New Zealand. I should have mentioned earlier that the TCCB, duly thankful for the backing of all their sponsors – and where would the game be without them? – must be especially delighted that Cornhill Insurance, now part of a vast German multi-national group, have yet again extended their support of English Test cricket.

It was an inspired hunch on the part of their manager, Cecil Burrows, when the Kerry Packer business blew up in 1977 and Cornhill leapt to England's rescue. Mr Burrows has never rued that decision. Nor, I am sure, has Fred Dinmore, who took detailed charge of the sponsorship's nuts and bolts.

Some of the things I have written about rugby have also been overtaken by events. I welcome the decision of the International Rugby Board to allow players and others to work gainfully for the media once their active careers are done, and regret only that its effect could not have been made retrospective to include some good and famous men willing but forever unable to serve the game in an official way.

The meeting at which that decision was made took place when the world of rugby union found itself rocked by the unofficial tour to South Africa of the so-called New Zealand Cavaliers, captained by Andy Dalton, coached by Colin Meads (an All Blacks selector) and managed by Ian Kirkpatrick. En route for a holiday in Durban, my wife and I touched down at Johannesburg airport shortly after the Cavaliers had flown in. When she bought the local *Sunday Times*, which carried a one-word banner headline, 'DEFIANT!', I naively enquired whether it referred to Mr Gaddafi's latest reaction to President Reagan. Not so. It merely described the snook being cocked at the establishment by Dalton's men. There could be no doubt we had arrived in the Republic.

It is ironic to reflect that the brouhaha would never have occurred – or at the least would have been postponed for a year – if the British Lions had toured South Africa in 1986 as scheduled. On the initiative of Dr Danie Craven, its president, the South African Board did not 'process' an invitation which must have been made privately at an earlier stage. Had that invitation been renewed, the home Unions, notably Scotland in a year when the Commonwealth Games were due in Edinburgh, would have had an agonizing decision to make. A vote to accept it, if not by the hefty majority manifested six years previously, would, I am sure, have been taken.

So it was left to the Cavaliers to fill South Africa's breech by accepting an invitation from the Transvaal. 'We are opening a door,' an unrepentant Colin Meads asserted in Johannesburg, 'that ought never to have been closed.' All but two of his Cavaliers had been chosen for a New Zealand tour of South Africa called off in 1985. One of those could not join the party in 1986 because his father was ill. There could be no doubt about the overall strength of the party, or of its conviction that a tour of South Africa was the apogee of their rugby careers.

John Reason and Clem Thomas, respectively correspondents of the *Sunday Telegraph* and *Observer*, flew in to report the rest of the tour just after I had watched the first international in Cape Town and then departed for a colder climate and some televised cricket. In a subsequent interview with Reason, published in the *Daily Telegraph*, Meads said: 'The game belongs to the players. Too many administrators never go near the players . . . When rugby administrators round the world consider the legal implications as carefully as we did, even more of them will back off . . . We are here as individuals exercising the right of individuals.'

Only seven of those were in South Africa with official approval. What an anguished New Zealand Union will do about the others is not, as I write, public news. Meads told Reason that he thought his whole party might be disciplined by being ruled out of consideration for the All Blacks team to play France in June. It would be very surprising if they were also to be banned from participation in rugby's first World

Cup competition, which is to be staged in Australia and New Zealand, with its final in Auckland, in our summer next year.

Whatever action the New Zealand Union may take it will not materially affect the tide of events if South African rugby is left officially in the cold. Administrators of the game in the northern hemisphere would be foolish to assume that they can isolate themselves from what is happening in the other. South African rugby has now thrown another spanner into the political works by inviting Australia to tour after the World Cup. There seems little doubt that if the Australian Union should decline the invitation, there will be no shortage of players, regardless of their government's attitude, who will be happy to follow the Cavaliers. Alan Jones, who coached the Wallabies to their grand slam in these islands in 1984, has been getting itchy feet.

In my old-fashioned way I hold that rugby's top players, who dedicate so much of their time, should be reimbursed for all their legitimate costs and generously entertained at their Unions' expense. *Ergo*, when players get paid to *play*, it will be a different ball game altogether.

Recent events in South Africa clearly have brought the threat of professional rugby union closer. I do not know whether New Zealand's Cavaliers have been given a nest-egg salted away in a Hong Kong bank or, as is more commonly supposed, been offered a substantial loan at a peppercorn rate of interest. Ian Kirkpatrick, a straight and honest man, has publicly and rigorously denied any such allegations.

As to the rugby I saw in South Africa, I can only say that anyone imagining that the Cavaliers had embarked on a goodwill, Barbarian-type tour was swiftly disillusioned. This, from the outset, was the genuine, red-blooded stuff, and the Republic's media had no qualms about the billing: South Africa v All Blacks, and no messing about.

Since the early departure from the active scene of the touring skipper, Andy Dalton, was only reported in these islands in brief and general terms, I am able to add a few unhappy details. Minutes into the opening match, Dalton was felled, his jaw broken, by a punch delivered from behind him by a flanker, Burger Geldenhuis, who was regarded as being strongly in contention for a place in the first international. The incident occurred many metres from the ball, so the referee could not be blamed for failure to see what happened. But it took place within a few metres of a touch judge who lamentably declined to draw the referee's attention to a blow distinctly more sickening than a number of others traded in that fixture and in others leading up to the first big trial of strength. Geldenhuis subsequently had the gall to state publicly that he would do it again if he had to, though he was sorry he had broken Dalton's jaw.

All credit to the South African public and its media, who were equally outraged by the incident. My old chum, Tony Venniker, a warm and natural broadcaster who is his country's 'Radio doctor', weighed in at the start of one of his weekly programmes with a suitable condemnation not just of the Geldenhuis punch but all the others as well. I suspect that Danie Craven interposed his authority to make certain that Geldenhuis was not chosen for the first international. In the herculean job he has done to sustain his Springboks at international level he has maintained the respect and admiration of many friends throughout the rugby world who must continue to stand by him now.

The first international was very fiercely but wholesomely fought out in driving rain, with the referee, Ken Rowlands of Wales, keeping a firm grip on affairs. There is a belief in the southern hemisphere, with which I agree, that northern arbitrators do not let the game flow enough, but this was a day of frequent handling mistakes and general errors. A touring side led by the redoubtable Andy Haden failed to develop the forward momentum in the loose which pessimistic home supporters had foreseen, and the Springboks' stand-off half and captain, Naas Botha, proved once more what a matchwinner he can be with his boot.

Having contributed three penalties and two dropped goals he sealed the result (21–15) at the climax, first with a diagonal kick to the left hand corner finished off by Carel du Plessis and then with a conversion from the touchline. But he had an off day as kicker in the second big match, in Durban, where it appears that the Cavaliers/All Blacks were a shade lucky but duly thankful to square the series (19–18) after an effort of typical determination and character. I have yet to be convinced that Botha is a great player in all respects but have no such reservation about the Springboks' centre, Danie Gerber, who is in the class of Bleddyn Williams, erstwhile of Wales. There can be no loftier praise.

Predicting the results of rugby matches, as I have often found, can be a dangerous occupation. Let me foolishly stick out my neck once more by suggesting that with (as I write this) two games to play, South Africa should win the series.

I imagine that I am not the only author of a book such as this who finally commits himself to print with the thought that he has left undone some of those things which he ought to have done. In my recollection of school days, I have somehow omitted to mention two popular young masters, Colin Silk and Philip Holtom, who made a special contribution to life at Cranbrook and were respected by all. Then there is Sheelagh O'Donovan, an Irish lady of irresistible warmth and unfailing good cheer who handled my business affairs throughout some happy years. I trust to be forgiven both by them and by others who may have yet stronger claims to jog an ailing memory.

Peter West
May 1986

Index

213

215

STAR BOOKS BESTSELLERS

	TESSA BARCLAY	
0352315520	**Garland of War**	£1.95
0352317612	**The Wine Widow**	£2.50
0352304251	**A Sower Went Forth**	£2.25
0352308060	**The Stony Places**	£2.25
0352313331	**Harvest of Thorns**	£2.25
0352315857	**The Good Ground**	£1.95
035231687X	**Champagne Girls**	£2.95
	JOANNA BARNES	
0352316969	**Silverwood**	£3.25
	LOIS BATTLE	
035231270X	**War Brides**	£2.75*
0352316640	**Southern Women**	£2.95*

STAR Books are obtainable from many booksellers and newsagents. If you have any difficulty tick the titles you want and fill in the form below.

Name _____

Address _____

_____

Send to: Star Books Cash Sales, P.O. Box 11, Falmouth, Cornwall, TR10 9EN.

Please send a cheque or postal order to the value of the cover price plus:
UK: 55p for the first book, 22p for the second book and 14p for each additional book ordered to the maximum charge of £1.75.

BFPO and EIRE: 55p for the first book, 22p for the second book, 14p per copy for the next 7 books, thereafter 8p per book.

OVERSEAS: £1.00 for the first book and 25p per copy for each additional book.

While every effort is made to keep prices low, it is sometimes necessary to increase prices at short notice. Star Books reserve the right to show new retail prices on covers which may differ from those advertised in the text or elsewhere.

*NOT FOR SALE IN CANADA

STAR BOOKS BESTSELLERS

STAR BOOKS BESTSELLERS

	CATHERINE COOKSON	
0426163524	**Hannah Massey**	£1.95
0352311339	**The Garment**	£1.95
0426163605	**Slinky Jane**	£1.95
	HENRY DENKER	
0352309601	**Horowitz and Mrs Washington**	£2.50*
0352303522	**The Experiment**	£1.95*
0352396067	**The Physicians**	£1.95*
0352312947	**Outrage**	£1.95*
0352316446	**Kate Kincaid**	£2.95*
	SUSANNAH CURTIS	
0352318376	**The Sad and Happy Years**	£2.95
	REGINE DEFORGES	
0352317930	**The Blue Bicycle**	£2.95

STAR Books are obtainable from many booksellers and newsagents. If you have any difficulty tick the titles you want and fill in the form below.

Name _____

Address _____

_____

Send to: Star Books Cash Sales, P.O. Box 11, Falmouth, Cornwall, TR10 9EN.

Please send a cheque or postal order to the value of the cover price plus:
UK: 55p for the first book, 22p for the second book and 14p for each additional book ordered to the maximum charge of £1.75.

BFPO and EIRE: 55p for the first book, 22p for the second book, 14p per copy for the next 7 books, thereafter 8p per book.

OVERSEAS: £1.00 for the first book and 25p per copy for each additional book.

While every effort is made to keep prices low, it is sometimes necessary to increase prices at short notice. Star Books reserve the right to show new retail prices on covers which may differ from those advertised in the text or elsewhere.

*NOT FOR SALE IN CANADA

STAR BOOKS BESTSELLERS

STAR BOOKS BESTSELLERS

DEAN R KOONTZ

0352319860	**Strangers**	£3.95*
035231950X	**The Vision**	£2.50*
035231608X	**Voice of The Night**	£2.25*
0352314796	**Darkness Comes**	£2.50*
0352309350	**Whispers**	£2.95*
0352301643	**Night Chills**	£3.25*
0352314400	**Shattered**	£1.80*
0352314370	**Phantoms**	£2.25*
0352314893	**Chase**	£1.95*

RAYMOND LEONARD

0352318201	**Nostradamus Inheritance**	£2.50*

GASTON LEROUX

0352317167	**The Phantom of the Opera**	£2.95

STAR Books are obtainable from many booksellers and newsagents. If you have any difficulty tick the titles you want and fill in the form below.

Name _____

Address _____

_____

Send to: Star Books Cash Sales, P.O. Box 11, Falmouth, Cornwall, TR10 9EN.

Please send a cheque or postal order to the value of the cover price plus:
UK: 55p for the first book, 22p for the second book and 14p for each additional book ordered to the maximum charge of £1.75.

BFPO and EIRE: 55p for the first book, 22p for the second book, 14p per copy for the next 7 books, thereafter 8p per book.

OVERSEAS: £1.00 for the first book and 25p per copy for each additional book.

While every effort is made to keep prices low, it is sometimes necessary to increase prices at short notice. Star Books reserve the right to show new retail prices on covers which may differ from those advertised in the text or elsewhere.

*NOT FOR SALE IN CANADA

STAR BOOKS BESTSELLERS

	JACK GERSON	
0352316187	**The Back of the Tiger**	£1.95
0352314672	**The Whitehall Sanction**	£1.95*
	ADAM HALL	
0352316071	**Northlight: A Quiller Mission**	£2.95*
	NOEL HYND	
0352319410	**Flowers from Berlin**	£3.25*
	ADAM KENNEDY	
0352313145	**The Domino Vendetta**	£1.80*
	MICHAEL KILIAN	
0352317574	**Blood of the Czars**	£2.25*
	HAROLD KING	
0352316314	**The Hahnemann Sequela**	£2.75*
	PETER LESLIE	
0352316683	**Death Mail**	£1.95

STAR Books are obtainable from many booksellers and newsagents. If you have any difficulty tick the titles you want and fill in the form below.

Name _____

Address _____

_____

Send to: Star Books Cash Sales, P.O. Box 11, Falmouth, Cornwall, TR10 9EN.

Please send a cheque or postal order to the value of the cover price plus:
UK: 55p for the first book, 22p for the second book and 14p for each additional book ordered to the maximum charge of £1.75.

BFPO and EIRE: 55p for the first book, 22p for the second book, 14p per copy for the next 7 books, thereafter 8p per book.

OVERSEAS: £1.00 for the first book and 25p per copy for each additional book.

While every effort is made to keep prices low, it is sometimes necessary to increase prices at short notice. Star Books reserve the right to show new retail prices on covers which may differ from those advertised in the text or elsewhere.

*NOT FOR SALE IN CANADA

STAR BOOKS BESTSELLERS

JOHN NORMAN

	THOMAS FLEMING	
0352316950	**The Spoils of War**	£3.95*
0352313986	**Dreams of Glory**	£2.95*
0352312750	**Promises to Keep**	£3.25*
0352310634	**The Officers' Wives**	£3.95*

ORDER FORM

STAR BOOKS are obtainable from many booksellers and newsagents. If you have any difficulty list the titles you want and fill in the form below:

TITLE   PRICE

_____

_____

_____

_____

_____

_____

_____

Name _____

Address _____

_____

Send to: Star Books Cash Sales, P.O. Box 11, Falmouth, Cornwall, TR10 9EN.

Please send a cheque or postal order to the value of the cover price plus:
UK: 55p for the first book, 22p for the second book and 14p for each additional book ordered to the maximum charge of £1.75.

BFPO and EIRE: 55p for the first book, 22p for the second book, 14p per copy for the next 7 books, thereafter 8p per book.

OVERSEAS: £1.00 for the first book and 25p per copy for each additional book.

While every effort is made to keep prices low, it is sometimes necessary to increase prices at short notice. Star Books reserve the right to show new retail prices on covers which may differ from those advertised in the text or elsewhere.

*NOT FOR SALE IN CANADA